BEHIND CLOSED DOORS

Behind
Closed Doors

Child abuse –
a survivor's story

Angus and Joanne Urquhart

Marshall Pickering
An Imprint of HarperCollins*Publishers*

Marshall Pickering is an Imprint of
HarperCollins*Religious*
Part of HarperCollins*Publishers*
77–85 Fulham Palace Road, London W6 8JB

First published in Great Britain
in 1993 by Marshall Pickering

1 3 5 7 9 10 8 6 4 2

A catalogue record for this book is
available from the British Library

ISBN 0 551 02502–6

Printed and Bound in Great Britain by
Cox & Wyman Ltd, Reading, Berkshire

To Jo

Acknowledgements

We would like to thank a number of people for the help they've given us while writing this book:

The Rev. Peter Timms – for all his love and encouragement.

Christine – for her patience in waiting for us to finish this book.

The Full Gospel Business Men's Fellowship – for their support.

Our pastor Colin – with thanks.

Linda Reeves – for her craziness, her love and her bullying to get this book done.

Denise Hewitson – for not only her support but also her love.

Our doctor Liz – for being more than just a doctor.

Ruby – for being a good friend to us and our son.

My cousin Colin – for being Colin.

John Sutton – for his kindness, frankness and honesty.

Johnny – for being gorgeous and the best.

1

To sift through the memories of a lifetime in order to write a book can be such a depressing and lonely task. From where I am now, to remember the pain and loneliness of my childhood is pain in itself. But when you know for sure that you have been chosen to survive, it can be rewarding. It would be hard for people to imagine me as I used to be, in fact, I have been told as much. The child I was then and the man I am becoming are entirely separate.

From the closed in, stifling hustle and bustle of inner-city London to the peaceful wide open spaces of the coast, things that other people take for granted, I have had to fight for. My wife, my family, I've had to fight to keep. I've had to fight very hard to keep my sanity at times. My pride has been shattered many times and my self-esteem has totally rejected me more times than I can remember. The pain of my childhood seemed to fuel a hatred and a desire to get even, not to let anyone beat me and it seemed to give me the strength to carry on.

My life seemed to consist of living behind closed doors that I didn't want opened by anyone. They were a barrier between a hostile world and myself, the fear and humiliation I felt were private, not to be shared.

My life now is about sharing and giving, not only taking as it used to be. The man who looks back at me in the mirror is now no longer a stranger, for my life is now an open book. I look forward to each new day, which is an experience I am still getting used to. I used to just survive; now I live.

My wife once told me one of the things that attracted her to me was my lost little boy look. I seemed lost and helpless, in such need of strong arms. In some ways I am still that little boy, I compare myself with my young son. Each day he learns something new, something exciting; we share that in common. Each day I learn something new, not only about myself but about the world around me. I spent so long in a world of darkness, full only of vice, drugs and violence that I was trapped; my world didn't develop from the time I was seven years old. For I didn't learn about the real world. As far as I was concerned, life consisted of drugs and the making and spending of money, no matter what the cost was to others. They were not important. If they got hurt I didn't care – that was life, that was my existence. Those doors I mentioned earlier have now been opened after three years of counselling, and I do not intend to allow them to close again.

Now they're open, I am beginning to realize that I have feelings and that they are very deep as well. Just walking along the cliffs with my family and our dogs, feeling the wind in my hair and on my face and to smell the sea. Freedom is a precious thing. Not only to be free but to *feel* free also can't be bad, can it? The mundane things in life like shopping with my wife to me are adventures into a world I've never had. All those goodies laid out, the sheer choice leaves me bewildered at times. After years of being out of prison it is still a novelty. I can buy and eat what I want. I don't have to go through a hotplate in prison. In there the food is laid out and you have two choices – eat it or go without. My main treat, though, is being free and I try hard to help others gain the freedom that I now enjoy; I pray every day that I am successful.

I have spent a lot of time with the Rev. Peter Timms, previously the governor of Maidstone prison. I used to see him as the man who held the keys to my freedom, a jailer. Little did I know, when I was in Maidstone all those years ago, that one day he would be instrumental in releasing me from my enforced mental prison. He is now our counsellor, spiritual adviser and friend.

When my wife and I first saw Peter as a counsellor three years ago, I thought, "a few months and he'll give us all the answers and we'll be fine". But it doesn't work like that, there are no packaged answers. We are pointed in the right direction and we find the answers ourselves. Only now, after three years, can I see the light at the end of the tunnel; pieces of my life and my emotions are being put together like a jigsaw. It has been very hard at times and very painful, but the rewards far outweigh any pain that is felt. There are no quick solutions. Problems that have taken years to build up are not going to be knocked down overnight and when I look back over these past three years I can now see the changes. Other people also help. We thank God that we are in a loving church where people care; being surrounded by understanding and loving people is a great bonus. They help to pick us up when we fall.

Joanne and I have come a long way since we met eight years ago. We have a comfortable house by the sea and we are content. We didn't always live like this, though. We started off in a top-floor flat on the

Downham Estate in Catford, southeast London, and we moved house approximately once a year for the first four years of marriage. The furniture we had in the beginning, what there was of it, nobody would have called comfortable. We moved to Margate four years ago. It's not luxury, you could hardly call an end-of-terrace, two-bedroomed house luxury, but it's a loving home and it's ours.

It's a far cry from where I was brought up in the borough of Bermondsey, southeast London. We lived in a tenement block in Sylvester Street. The borough is situated in the Elephant and Castle – near the south side of London Bridge – where Charlie Chaplin was born. It was a bombed-out, rat-infested place, a leftover wreck from World War Two. All around us were bombed-out buildings, piles of rubble that we were told never to play on. None of the children ever listened and there were always accidents – some fatal. This soon became a part of life for me.

The block we lived in was owned by a private landlord who was not famous for carrying out repairs to his properties. The building was damp and decaying, the rubbish chutes ran right down the centre of the building and into the cellar where we used to catch rats. My mother used many bottles of disinfectant to quell the stink of the rotting rubbish.

My family moved down from Aberdeen, Scotland when I was just a year old. There wasn't much decent accommodation around in the days just after the war. So when they came to London they had to take what they could find. The flat was bright and cheerful, with thick carpets on the floor, fires in every room to keep the damp down, warm curtains and brightly coloured paper on the walls. Home, as I chose to remember it was a cosy and loving place, like a haven in a swamp. But in reality it was part of the swamp. The violence that was commonplace in Bermondsey at the time was also a major part of my home life, but I painted a picture of domestic happiness to my friends and even to myself. When you are told something often enough as a child you begin to believe it. I was told I had got it wrong, things weren't that bad. If I spoke about the violence to anyone I was told I was lying, so consequently I began to believe that they were right and I was wrong. My mind blocked out the bad memories of my father who had a terrible drink problem and was not averse to indulging in violent rows with my mother who drank too much at times also. In remembering the realities of my childhood I have realized that the love I was shown after a row or drinking binge was out of guilt. I would be rewarded with gifts, days out and lots of affection. I resented this; it was as though they were trying to buy my forgiveness. When I approached them for reassurance I was told that it wouldn't happen again and I always hoped they were right. It wouldn't be long, though, before they were at it again and I would bury my head in my pillow while biting my lip, wishing they'd stop. There were times when I gathered the courage and attempted to stop the arguments, only to get in the way of their flying fists and feet. My pain was ignored and they reacted angrily telling me to get back to bed. It was as if they were only interested in the moment and not me. I would return to my room but the noise followed me, I couldn't get away from it. My escape was our back yard. With my blanket around me and my dog beside me, for a time I could escape from their world and fall into a troubled sleep till the quietness would awaken me and I knew it was safe to go back to bed. The thing that hurt most was that they didn't seem to miss me; they never came looking for me.

I had a secret camp that was about twenty feet below the ground; it was part of an old bank vault. To us children, this was like an adventure playground where we rambled over and explored the surrounding ruins never realizing the dangers. The people in the area were what I liked most. They would rob an outsider blind and smile while they were doing it, but in all adversities they were cheerful.

I have one childhood memory that sticks in my mind. I was about four when my eldest brother Soult got married – he was sixteen years older than me. I went with my parents and brothers, seven of us in all, to visit his girlfriend's family. I was fascinated by her father who had a wart on the end of his nose – my father had told me that people with warts on their noses had looked through too many keyholes. So I, in all innocence, asked him how many he had looked through. My mother was not amused and gave me a clip round the ear for being rude.

Later, their younger daughter, one of my brothers and I went out to play. I remember she kept wanting to kiss me, which annoyed my brother because she wouldn't take any notice of him. He picked up a lump of wood and threw it at me, so I picked up a milk bottle and threw it at him; it broke and cut his leg. He ran in to my mother and told her what I had done. She came out and was just about to tick me off when the little girl told her he was lying, that he had kicked the bottle and it had broken. So he received a good telling off and I had my first girlfriend. This little romance lasted all of two weeks, then she said that we should go steady and get married – at four years old it was a bit of a prospect, wasn't it? I told her I was too young to settle down with a wife and that I wanted to play the field a bit. I didn't know what it meant but I had heard my brothers say it and it sounded good. She told me I was a tease and a flirt, and that we were finished. So ended my first romance.

These early years of my life at times were very happy. I realized very early that I didn't like school and quite often used to slip out the back way to play on the bomb sites locally. There were three of us who used to "hang around" together at that time. We would fight mock battles with each other. Tony and Vic came from poor families, so we started stealing from local shops and the big East End market. I was the decoy. As my father was a local businessman, nobody suspected us and we got away with it every time.

So came my baptism into crime. Little did I know then that these small crimes were going to cost me so much pain in the future and years in prison. But innocent as our petty theft seemed at the time, there was, crouching at the door, lying in wait for me, an event that would destroy my childhood forever.

2

The change in my life came on my seventh birthday. It is not a day that I have fond memories of. Rather, I look back on it with horror. A day that would shatter my life as I knew it.

My seventh birthday came and like all the birthdays before it I fell asleep the night before full of excitement, wondering what presents my mum and dad had bought for me. I was hoping for a bike.

I awoke in the morning, jumped out of bed, ran to the front door and was disappointed not to see any birthday cards. Then I remembered – it was only six o'clock in the morning. Mum and Dad were already up as were my five brothers.

My mother gave me a big box, and I wondered, how on earth they could get a bike in a box like that. When I opened it I realized it wasn't a bike but a train set. I received lots of small presents – but no bike.

I was disappointed because I longed for one. So my father sat me on his knee and explained that I was a bit too young and too small to have one – I was very short for my age. Maybe next year, he told me.

My disappointment didn't last long, though, with the arrival of the postman bringing my birthday cards. My sister had sent me one from Scotland. She was quite a bit older than me and when we all moved to London she had wanted to stay, so she lived with our grandparents in Dundee. I loved my sister dearly and she always made a fuss of me when I went to stay with her in the school holidays. She would take me to the fair and other places that boys of my age loved to go. So I was excited to see what present she had bought me. I opened her card and tucked inside was a postal order for seven shillings and sixpence, which in those days was a small fortune to me. My mum said I should take it to the post office and put it into my savings book until I decided what to buy with it. So off I went down the road to the post office. On the way I decided to treat myself, so I put the seven shillings into my savings book and kept sixpence to spend. I asked the man in the post office to give me sixpence in half pennies so I had twelve coins to jingle in my pocket. I felt really grown up.

I decided to look around the shops. My mum had packed some sandwiches as I had told her I would be spending the day with Tony and Vic, two of my friends, in the park. The first shop I looked in was the bike shop. There in the window was my dream bike, all shiny new paint and chrome. I wanted that bike so much.

I heard a voice behind me; it was Gino, a local shop-keeper. "Didn't you get your bike then, Angus?" he said. I turned round and told him I hadn't and what my dad had said. He gave me a pat on the head and a new shilling and told me not to worry. He said if I promised to do as I was told and not tell anyone, I could go round to his shop that afternoon and he would let me ride his shop bike. But it must be our secret, he said. So I promised not to tell anyone. I felt quite pleased with myself. I now had one shilling and sixpence, I was also going to ride a bike, and a grown-up's bike at that. I couldn't wait for one o'clock to come so I could go round to Gino's and ride his bike.

I had a few hours to kill so I carried on looking in the shops. I went into Woolworths to look at some of the toys. While I was looking I noticed a little blue wind-up van, but the price was over a shilling and that would've made a big dent in my money. (I was a shrewd kid, always out to make money wherever I could and didn't like spending it if I didn't have to.) I wanted this little van so I looked around me, slipped it into my schoolbag along with my sandwiches, thinking no one had seen me and walked out of the shop.

I went to Tabard Park, which was just over the back from where we lived. It was surrounded on three sides by tenement blocks; the north side of the park was a bomb site where a school had stood before it was blown up during the war and we used to play there now and then.

When I got to the park I took out my new van. I wound it up and watched it trundle off all on its own. I thought it was great and how clever I had been in stealing it. My mum wouldn't notice one more toy as I had lots of new toys.

It was getting on for twelve thirty by now, so I hurried out of the park to get to Gino's by one o'clock. As I walked down the road I picked up stones and skated them along the ground. One bounced a little too high and went straight through a lady's window. As I ran off, I remember her shouting after me, "God will punish you for your wickedness." Silly old woman, I thought, anyone would think I'd robbed a bank instead of just breaking a window.

Later on, though, those words shouted in anger at me would haunt me for years to come. From that day on I was to be at war with God.

I had always thought of God as being a loving God who cared for people. Or at least that's what I'd been taught at school as well as at home. The kind man who looks down on earth and is somewhat detached from what the majority of people are going through.

What was to happen to me later on that day really made me hate God. He was getting his own back as far as I was concerned for breaking that window. I reached Gino's shop – for once I was early – normally I was late for everything. I knocked on the door. I was getting butterflies in my stomach, for it was something I had wanted to do for a long time. Gino opened the door and told me to go through to the back room. I knew the way. I had been there many times before. It was, in fact, a storeroom cum sitting room at the back of the shop. Gino or his wife could sit there and relax and keep an eye on the store.

He came in and offered me a drink of orange or lemonade. I accepted orange. To this day I still hate orange. I asked where his wife was. He explained that she was out shopping. I drank my orange, eager to learn how to ride this bike.

I noticed some photographs on the table – they were pictures of nude men and women. I had seen pictures like these before in school and my brothers used to hide them in their bedrooms and I knew all their hiding places. I just thought they were the kind of things that grown-ups looked at, so it didn't really bother me But there were also some here with men and young boys in them. They surprised me somewhat because I hadn't seen pictures like that before. I asked Gino what they were doing and he said they were playing. I accepted this to a certain extent because I'd had to "play games" like this with my father and brothers and as far as I was concerned grown-ups were a bit strange at times. Anyway I was more interested in learning to ride the bike. I asked him where the bike was and he led me out into the back yard. Enclosing it was a brick wall and the yard was half covered overhead with canvas, the other half was covered with wire mesh glass shading it from the sun. Gino switched on the overhead light and there, resting on its stand was the bike. It was a big old bike with a large basket on the front for carrying groceries to customers. He lifted me onto the saddle and if I really stretched I could just about touch the pedals. I was very wobbly sitting there, stretching forward to reach the handlebars. Gino said it would be better if he tied my hands to the handlebars to stop me toppling off. I was perfectly relaxed with this so I let him do it. I told him, though, that I wasn't very comfortable as I had to stretch so far forward that my backside was right up off the saddle. He went away and came back with a cushion and put it under me. I was quite happy sitting there now, racing races in my mind and of course I was winning them. It felt terrific to be so grown-up. Then he handed me two white sweets and told me they would help me to ride the bike better, that all grown-ups who raced bikes took them. He knew that I wanted to be the same as them so he put them in my mouth and gave me a drink to wash them down with.

Years later I found that what he had given me was a very addictive relaxant drug. My eyes started to get heavy and I was feeling very drowsy. I felt Gino take my trousers and pants off. I remember thinking it must be bedtime – my mum quite often undressed me and put me to bed. My last thought was what a nice day it had been. Then he raped me. I couldn't understand what was happening to me. Nobody had done this to me before. The "games" I had played with my father weren't like this. To this day I still remember the pain. I remember other acts that were done to me and I remember being sick. I must've passed out because the next thing I remember I was lying on a bed and something nice and cold was being put on my face. I thought I must have had a bad dream, until I opened my eyes.

Sitting there next to me was Gino; he was smiling at me. Then pain seemed to wash over me in waves. I started to cry, and told him I was going to tell my mum. He smiled, then he slapped me really hard. I was totally shocked and it stopped me crying. I couldn't understand why I was being treated like this. Every time I'd cried before, adults would cuddle and comfort me. He told me he'd seen me steal the little van and that it had to be our secret because if I told my mum and dad what had happened, not only would he tell them I'd stolen it but he would also tell the police and they would lock me up in prison. He took great pleasure in telling me what a dark, horrible place it was, a place where you are beaten up time and again and where the only food they gave you was bread and water. I became really scared at this. I was terrified, for I had friends whose fathers were in prison and they'd told me that's what the prisons were like when they had visited them.

Gino told me what had happened to me was normal and showed me photos of other children and asked me if I thought they looked happy. I said they did and he told me I'd get to like doing things like this because when I did well he would give me lots of nice things, but if I was bad he would punish me.

He then wanted me to perform another act, but I said no. He slapped me again and I did what he told me. Afterwards, he gave me a brand new pound note. I had never had a whole pound note all to myself before – it was a fortune.

I told him I was feeling tired, so he gave me what he called sherbet. All of a sudden I felt really good, full of life and energy. I now know it was amphetamine.

He asked me if I was going to keep our secret. I asked him if he was going to tell anyone about the van. He said he wouldn't, so I promised not to say anything. I told him I would have to go and he helped me get dressed. I was surprised to find that the pain had receded and he said that was because of the "sweets" he had given me and if it came back, I was to go and see him and he would give me some more. I smiled and said I didn't think it would come back as I was better. He just smiled knowingly and gave me some in a bag to take away. I thought this time was no different from when I had hurt myself at home. My mother would make it better and it would stay better.

Little did I know that those "sweets" taken in innocence were to lead me onto the downward slippery slopes of drug addiction that was to go on for over thirty years and was to be a contributing factor that would put me in prison, not once, but three times.

I reached out to pick up my little van, but Gino got there first. He picked it up with a cloth and put it into a bag. He said he would keep it as long as I did as I was told. If not, it would go to the police.

Just then the cupboard door opened and out stepped his wife – she had seen and heard everything. She took the bag off him and told me she would look after it. I felt as though I was going to cry, but I stopped myself. I swore inwardly that nobody would ever make me cry again.

Even now, after all these years, I still find it nearly impossible to cry, so deep was the pain buried. I know that one day, though, I will be blessed with the capability to share in the release valve of other men.

As I left, his wife called after me and told me to be a good boy and God would take care of me. It was then I remembered what the other lady had shouted at me, that God would punish me for being a bad boy and breaking her window. I vowed I would not only go to war with this person called God, but that one day I would kill Gino. But I was only small so it would have to wait. I left feeling quite pleased with myself. Not only did I have lots of money on me, and there was lots more where that came from, but one day I would fix God and Gino.

I made my way to the "hide" – it was still only two thirty. An hour and a half had gone by but it seemed like a lifetime. I was never going to be the same again.

The "hide" was my secret place. It was in the ruins of an old bank. The building had been bombed but there was a brick wall surrounding it. I used to climb over the wall and go down to what used to be the cellars. They were big places and there was a hole in the wall I used to climb through and down an old brick staircase to what used to be the bank vault. I would light my candles and I was home. I felt safe here. This is where I came if I wanted to be on my own. I had an old armchair, carpets and even a little camping stove.

I sat down there that day and screamed in pain. It was like a huge burning flame that seemed to shoot right through me. I shot to my feet, then fell to my hands and knees – this seemed the most comfortable position to be in. How long I was there in that position I don't know. I didn't know what had been done to me. I only knew I was in terrible pain. It was then I made my mind up that I was going to get Gino, I didn't know how, for I was only small and in a stand-up fight I could never win.

I took my trousers off; they were bloodstained. Despite my vow, I started to cry and was just about to put them on again and go and tell my mum what had happened to me when I remembered what Gino had said about the police. So I decided I had better clean them up as best I could. It was then I remembered the pills he had given me. They had got rid of the pain before so I took them. There I was seven years old and on the way to becoming a drug addict – lovely world we live in, isn't it?

Just as before, the pain started to go away. I started to laugh, I didn't know why, but I could not seem to stop. I dipped my trousers into a puddle, rinsed them off and patched myself up as best I could. I was to bleed for nearly two weeks afterwards. I put my trousers on, still laughing – everything was so funny – even the way the water rippled in the puddle.

I threw my pants away, put my trousers back on and sat down gingerly. It was O.K., the pain had gone completely. I started to wonder how I could get this guy. I remembered an old friend of my father's – he had been an Irish "freedom fighter" and he used to sit for hours and tell me about the violence he'd been involved in – the acts of revenge against the British. He'd explained that these acts had been carried out secretly so as to avoid imprisonment. He told me of an incident where a house had been burned down and explained in great detail how it had been carried out. My eyes fell on a can of petrol in the corner. I smiled to myself nervously, wondering if this would be a good idea. I decided to carry out my plan later. I picked up the can of petrol, made my way home and hid it in my parents' back yard.

As soon as I walked in my mother asked me if I was all right. I told her I was tired because it had been a busy day. I knew she didn't believe me. For a moment I panicked, then I remembered the lady whose window I had broken. I told her about it and that it was an accident, but I was worried because I thought she would punish me. She gave me one of her smiles which told me everything was O.K. She held her arms out and I ran to her for a cuddle. I felt bad because of what had happened to me: I started to sob really hard but there were no tears. I really wanted to tell her but I was too frightened. She asked again what else was wrong, but I just gave her a kiss and told her I was happy.

She led me into the kitchen and there on the table was a birthday cake and all the family were invited to my birthday tea. My brothers and their wives came over and the party was great but, as always, I ate too much and felt sick. But I had enjoyed myself so much that I'd almost forgotten the ordeal I'd gone through earlier that day – it seemed to recede to the depths of my mind, venturing forward slowly until I pushed it back again.

One of my sisters-in-law asked me if I wanted to spend the night at their flat, which was directly above my parents'. I was about to say yes – I enjoyed staying with them – when I remembered what I was going to do to Gino that night. So I asked if I could leave it until the next night. I told them I wanted to stay in my own bedroom surrounded by my new toys. They agreed and I was sent off to bed with the promise of a story from my dad. I went apprehensively, not knowing what mood he would be in. He came into the bedroom with a beaming smile on his face. I knew this was going to be a happy story and not one of his "games". He was a huge man, over twenty stone, an ex-bare-fist fighter, but at times he was very gentle. He would tease me and ask which story I wanted and I would shake my head at each one. Then he would get up off the bed and say, "O.K., if you don't want a story—" Then I would pick one. I don't think I ever heard the endings as I always fell asleep.

I awoke with a start and lay there wondering what had woken me up. There was only the glow from the fire throwing dancing fingers down the wall. Then I felt the pain coming back. I squeezed my eyes shut hoping it would go away, but it seemed to get worse. I looked across at my elder brother lying next to me – we slept in a big double bed with an old feather mattress – it was always a cosy bed. All I could see of him was the top of his head and I knew he was asleep, so I eased out of bed and stood up. I remembered Gino at this point and with the pain I was feeling I was now wide awake.

I hoped it was not too late as my mum was always up and about at five a.m. to do her early morning cleaning job. I looked at the clock. It was ten past two, so there was time. I smiled to myself. Gino, your time has come, I thought. I slipped on my trousers and my jumper over the top of my pyjamas, put on my shoes and I was ready. Creeping out of the bedroom I listened; there wasn't a sound, so I went into the kitchen and gathered up a cloth, petrol and a box of matches as my dad's Irish friend had told me. I made my way into the living room by the light of the fire and carefully easing the window open so as not to make a sound, I climbed out. I was going to use this way many times in the future to keep appointments in my life of drugs and porn.

I made my way to Gino's shop, went round to the back and looked up at the windows. All was in darkness. The moon wasn't out so I could hardly see. I went to the back door and knelt down, felt in my pocket for the matches, then poured the petrol over the rag. I had never felt such hatred before as I did that night for the man who had raped me. I wanted him dead.

Match after match blew out as I attempted to light the rag. I knelt down, sheltering the rag between my feet and tried again. It suddenly burst into flames. My joy turned to terror when I realized that petrol had spilled onto a shoe as well and that was burning better than the rag. There I was, matches in one hand, burning rag in the other, dancing around trying to stamp out the fire on my shoe. My foot was getting really hot by now. I remember thinking, how come this never happened to my dad's Irish friend – he always seemed to get it right first time.

Then I remembered the water tap which was attached to the wall; it was used for cleaning. I could see it from the light of my burning shoe and I hopped over to it as quickly as I could. My foot was really painful by now and in my desperation it took me longer to turn it on and I was finding it harder to balance on one leg. The water, when it finally hit my foot, felt like heaven. Now, along with my other pains, I also had a burnt foot. I screamed in temper, then remembered where I was. I stood still for a few moments and listened, but no sound came. Nobody had heard me.

I went back to the back door of Gino's shop. There was a little window at the side of the door that was open slightly. I pulled it and it opened enough for me to climb in. I made my way into the back room of the shop. I was really in pain now; it seemed to ride over me in waves. I sat down at the table and looked around me. The cupboard Gino had taken the pills out of was standing in the corner. I decided I would take some as the pain was getting unbearable. I went over to the cupboard. There on the shelf was the pill jar. My heart sank – there was only one left. I took it and put the bottle back. Next to it was a brown envelope. I picked it up and looked at it. There was something inside and thinking it might be something valuable, I slipped it into my pocket.

The rag was burned up by now so I decided to use the petrol on its own. I went out to the yard and picked up the petrol can, then went back in and sprinkled the petrol all round the room as I had seen it done in the films. I made a trail to the back door and stood there for a while, thinking about what I was going to do. Suppose they found out it was me. Then I thought, they would never suspect a nice little boy like me of starting a fire. I smiled to myself.

I lit a match, set light to the petrol, made sure it was burning, then put the can against the wall. I wanted Gino to know it was done on purpose. It burnt really well, then I ran all the way home.

I was surprised to learn it was ten past four. I didn't realize I'd been gone that long. I crept back into my bedroom and undressed. I hid my shoes as I didn't know what to do about them. I would work that one out tomorrow. I hid the envelope in my secret place behind the skirting board and crept back into bed. I was so tired I fell into a deep sleep. I'd had a busy day. There were to be many just like it.

The following day, everyone was talking about the shop that burnt out the night before. My brother told me about huge fire engines and police cars that had been called to the scene. I started to get worried. Then my dad told me whose shop it was and that as far as they knew it was caused by a gas leak. I was relieved, but at the same time displeased because I wanted Gino to know it was me. I was told that Gino and his wife were both O.K. and again I was displeased. I made up my mind I was going to get the pair of them another time.

That day I didn't go to school. My mother thought I had a temperature so she arranged for the neighbours to pop in and out to keep an eye on me. While I was lying in bed after my mum had gone to work, I remembered the brown envelope I'd taken. There were photos in it like the ones I'd seen the day before and I was surprised that a girl in one of them was someone I knew from school. Her name was Tracey and she was a year older than me. The man (I found out later he was a very influential person) was doing to her what had been done to me.

It shocked me but also reinforced the feeling that it was normal behaviour. I didn't fully know what was going on, as sex at that time was not spoken about at all. But I did know that I didn't like it so I assumed she didn't either.

Just then there was a knock on the door. It was Tracey. She told me she knew what had happened to me. I found out later that she had been sent round by Gino to make everything look attractive, to woo me if you like. She told me of all the good things we could get out of these people – the money, days off school (one of our teachers was involved), outings to different places etc. I told her about the "hide", and she came to see it with me.

We used this place for years to store our money, away from grown-ups who would ask questions. That day we started a partnership together that would last for many years. Tracey pulled me out of many a tight spot later on, but most importantly, she taught me how to survive.

She told me that her father had introduced her to sex at the age of six. He kept her quiet by telling her that nobody would believe her. I asked her if it was right what I'd been told, about the toy van I'd stolen. She said yes, her father was a magistrate and he knew lots of policemen. She said the grown-ups liked to "play games". I was to "play games" like these many times in the ensuing years – with policemen, shopkeepers, judges, people whose public and private lives never came close to meeting. I found out a lot that afternoon: we spoke for hours that day. I told her everything that had happened, and she told me. She became my girl-friend and my lover that day and from then on we were inseparable.

When I look back at those early years of my life, I find myself wondering – if I had not been raped and so badly abused for so many years, would I have turned out to be a different kind of person? I am discovering that I would not. If I had not faced up to the abuse on myself and the way in which I abused others, then I would not have changed. But in facing my early life with honesty, I find that the person coming out now is the man I would have been. Yes I have anger at what I have lost, for I was a clever child. I could have been a doctor or so many things, but I'm not. I'm an ex-con. I used to look at those bad years as lost, but now I realize they are a wealth of experience that I can use. I have had a meeting with someone called Jesus. He showed me that my life had a purpose and in sharing my experiences I could show that as far as God is concerned no one is a lost cause. So you see God has a place in my life's experiences.

I find recently that more and more I'm thinking about my mum and dad. What kind of parents were they? How did they seem to me then? Were they outwardly loving or "cardboard" parents going through the motions? Did they have any idea that their child had been raped and abused and closed their eyes to it like so many other parents do? These questions I will never have answers to as my parents died a long time ago.

I've found through experience that many parents sus-pect abuse involving their children, but the suspicion alone is so painful to them that they block it out and in doing so ignore the child's pain. When the child is older and can understand what has happened to him or her and they tell their parents or a relative, it is devastating to find out that they knew, or that they had an idea of what was going on. I was speaking to a member of my family not so long ago and I told him a bit about my childhood, how I was raped and who had done it. He didn't seem surprised at what had happened, only at who it was. I got the feeling that he knew all about it. I was so inwardly angry with him, I could not believe that he could've known and yet said or done nothing about it. When we left his house, my wife told me to pull the car over.

She spoke my thoughts and then told me not to hate him, for that was how you were raised, not to speak of bad things. I cried that night, but with her arms around me it made all the difference. It opened a door in me. I was brought up like that, but it was then I began to ask myself the question, What were my parents really like?

My wife reminded me of her dad's reaction when she told him she had been abused. He had said he'd had an idea something wasn't right, but, well, that was water under the bridge now. Just a figure of speech, an unthinking reaction but that was how he had been raised, no different to my family. Yes, it was water under the bridge, but my wife was still trapped in that stream. Even today the subject is not broached unless my wife or I bring it up. Then we are listened to but no questions are asked. The "brush it under the carpet" syndrome does not help anyone, does it? And it causes so much pain.

When I think of my parents, I realize I hardly knew

them. As Mum and Dad I did, but as fellow human beings I didn't. There always seemed to be a wall between us and some things were never spoken about. I was told not to be a baby if I cried when I hurt myself. But I *was* a baby. Feelings were not spoken about, ever. I know now my parents were products of their time. I was always told I had to do as my elders said, not to answer back or question them for they knew best. Respect is one thing, blind obedience is something else. I am trying to teach my little boy not always to obey grown-ups – they can be wrong. He is encouraged to question everything he doesn't understand. He is also taught that respect has to be earned as does trust. The confusing double standards of my childhood; like, don't answer your elders back no matter what, speak only when you're spoken to, children should be seen and not heard; have all gone out of the window in my household. Looking back now, I realize that this attitude to children was one of the reasons why my abuse didn't come to light. I was doing what I had been taught to do; my elders knew best. I was doing as I was told. I had nobody to turn to.

Don't get me wrong; they were affectionate. I believe they loved me in their own way, but it was not in the way I needed. I had plenty of hugs and kisses from my mother but she never actually spoke to me; she was Mum and I was only the child. There was never any thought given to the fact that one day I would become an adult and parent and I needed to be prepared for that.

My father was the head of the family and he was a distant person. He put bread and butter on the table, but there was always a hardness there. He gave cuddles, they both did, but looking back, there were many times that I wondered if they really loved me. When I asked them, their reply was "of course we do". If I asked for a cuddle I got one, but I always had to approach them. I needed to know I was loved, then perhaps I would've exposed what had happened to me while they were still alive.

My parents had faults, but then so do everyone's; they did things wrong, but then as a father so will I. I'll make mistakes, but I hope I will admit them and try to put them right. We don't want our son growing up with the idea that Mum and Dad are perfect.

I didn't have the chance to make my peace with my parents, but I have a chance in a way to put that right. I didn't like my in-laws when I first met them – they were so like my parents – same values and outlook on life. But as my values have changed and I've become calmer, I find I really do love and care for them. They're O.K. They may not give me hugs and kisses or tell me they love me, but then it's early days isn't it? I feel that with them I have been given another chance, that God in His own way has given me another mum and dad, so I will try to do better second time around.

3

The Gino episode changed my life drastically as you can imagine. I became more aggressive towards members of my family, in particular one of my brothers, and some of our fights became very violent. I went from being a happy, carefree child, to being very quiet, withdrawn and sometimes moody. I had lots of friends in school before this event; afterwards I had none and the ones I did have I lost because of my moods.

I became a loner. I felt alone, as if it was me against the world and the world was winning hands down. I formed a plan of battle and in doing so I retreated and closed the door to the outside world.

I started to put all the bad things that happened to me onto an imaginary friend called John. He was the one they hurt. He cried, I didn't. I became detached from it all.

I had vowed never to cry again and I didn't. Inside I cried like mad, huge body-racking tears, but outside, never a tear. I started to win. I was beating these people, but at what cost to me? As a human being it destroyed me. I failed to be a normal member of the human race. I had no feelings, no love.

I blamed my parents for not protecting me and my attitude towards them changed. I answered my father back, argued all the time, played my mother off against my father. I started stealing from them then blamed one of my brothers. When caught I would offer no explanation. I was caught out in some horrendous lies yet insisted I was telling the truth.

When I was seven and a half years old, I started to masturbate, sometimes when I knew my parents would catch me. It became so bad they took me to see a specialist at Guy's hospital. Upon examination, the only thing the doctor said to my mother was that I had developed early. This was all within six months of the first rape. I say first because it was repeated over and over. I started in child prostitution and was introduced into a porn ring.

The point I'm trying to make is that all these changes in behaviour were my way as a child of telling my parents that things were not right. When they failed to notice my cries for help, a hatred built up towards them that went on for many years. So look to your children and if they give you signs that something is wrong, if their behaviour changes, it may be nothing but puberty, but then again it may be something far more sinister. Whatever reason, listen to them. You can learn so much from just a few little words or even a drawing. Put the child's feelings first and yours to one side and by doing this, the insight and understanding will come that will enable you to help them overcome any major hurdle in their lives.

I began to realize that I wasn't the only one. There were many many more like me. I was asked if I wanted to meet a real live television star – this man even had his own programme. I accepted the invitation. I was to find out from first-hand experience that Gino and Tracey's dad weren't the only users in this twilight world.

I got up the second morning feeling much better. As long as I didn't move too quickly, the pain was bearable. I went to school with my friends Tony and Vic and on the way I told them that I would be hopping the wag from school and told them not to say anything. They asked me where I was going, so I told them it was my business what I did. Before I knew it, it was lunchtime. Tracey had told me about the meeting with the TV star and I was to meet her round the corner from the school. Mr Richardson, our teacher, would meet us there. I was told not to be late as he had to be back for afternoon school.

We went by taxi. I was excited as I had never been in one before, nor had I been in a big posh house either. Mr Richardson didn't seem the same to me that day; he was ever so jumpy. I sat in the front on my own while Tracey and the teacher sat in the back talking quietly. I couldn't hear what was being said but Tracey leaned over and whispered to me that we had to stop off first at the teacher's house, but not to worry as it was on the way. I asked why and she said that we had to play some games with him to pay for the taxi and also for the time off school. I must have looked worried because she told me everything would be all right.

We arrived at his house and there we had to perform acts of sex with him. It was over with very quickly and we were soon dressed and on our way to meet this star.

The house was extremely large from the outside. As we travelled up the long winding driveway and the house came into view I thought, wow, wait till I tell Mum, Dad and my brothers about this. Tracey seemed to read my thoughts and told me to remember that it was our secret and nobody must know or we would get into serious trouble.

I didn't know what she meant by "serious trouble" but it began to dawn on me that I was being trapped. I knew I didn't have a choice so I complied anyway, deciding however to tell my dog, Butch. I told him all my secrets and he always kept them. We received payment for our exploits, two pounds from Mr Richardson – it seemed like a fortune. Tracey told me we would also get five pounds each from the television person. I could not believe it – seven pounds in one afternoon. We were rich. Seven pounds in those days was more than most working-class people got in one week's wages and here I was with that amount in a couple of hours. Money was to play a big part in my life from then on.

I didn't know until about six months later that the whole afternoon had been carefully planned. The incident at the teacher's house had been to get me ready and to put me at ease for what was to come. I'm sorry to say, looking back on it now, that their plan worked. There was once a part of me that couldn't understand why I didn't say no more often and why I didn't put a stop to it but allowed it to go on. I've realized now that even as adults we go along with things we know to be wrong. Is it because we fear punishment or pain, or is it because we fear the ridicule of not being listened to? I believe that all these reasons played a major part in me not "going public". It was the fear of what they would do to me, but also I didn't think I would be believed. In fact as I got older I was proved right. Tracey had told me that if I told the truth but did it with a laugh I would not be believed. I tried it. Part of me deep down wanted to be believed but there was another part of me that was greatly relieved when I wasn't and I was accused of living in a fantasy world.

We pulled up at the house. It looked gigantic to me at that time. As soon as the taxi stopped the door opened as if magically and there stood the celebrity. I was to get to know him quite well over the years. I was ushered into a huge hall which was as big as the little flat we lived in. There was a large marble staircase to one side of the hall that led up to the next floor. It seemed so big and grand to my young eyes. There was even a huge chandelier hanging from the ceiling just like in the films. It looked as though the whole house was straight out of a film. I wondered how anyone could have so much money to own such a big house. It had gardens and lawns at the back that led down to the river; there was even a cruiser tied up at a pier. I would visit many such houses as I got older. Eventually I accepted them as just a part of life.

After a few words with our host, who I will call Jim, our teacher left. Jim told Tracey to show me around the house then to take me to the playroom (which was actually a very large dining room). I followed Tracey round that house with my mouth and eyes wide open in wonder. There was a gym and swimming pool in the cellar, bathrooms with baths so big you could swim in them easily. He had large mirrors on the walls in nearly every room. Tracey told me she would show me something. She pressed a button at the side of a mirror and it opened. She took my hand and we stepped inside. She closed the mirror and told me to look round. I was amazed. I was looking out into the room we'd just left, yet from the other side it looked just like an ordinary mirror. She told me it was called a two-way mirror and explained what it was used for. She also told me that they used it for taking photos and making films. I'd never seen anything like this before. Just then a bell rang and Tracey said it was time to go, Jim would be waiting for us. She took my hand and led me to the "playroom".

It was a huge room, with large mattresses laid out in a square and a larger one in the middle. There were lights set around the room to highlight the middle mattress. The rest of the room was in darkness. It reminded me of the films that were set in Roman times. I'd only ever seen things like this in the films, never in real life. It amazed me. I became aware that there were other people in the room, apart from Tracey, Jim and myself. There were five other men, plus two young girls and a boy. The girls were a few years older than Tracey, about fourteen; their names were Nikki and Joan. The boy's name was Jason. I felt a bit out of place because nobody else had any clothes on. To see so much naked flesh in one room for the first time was a bit overpowering. Tracey and Nikki led me to the mattress in the middle of the room. Nikki gave me a hanky and told me to inhale into it. It was a sticky sweet smell, not unpleasant. I soon found that I was feeling very drowsy. I seemed to feel hands all over me. It reminded me of what had happened in Gino's shop. I felt terrified but helpless to do anything about it. Then I felt a cool hand stroking me and a gentle voice speaking to me. I don't know what was said but it seemed to calm me.

I do know that there were unspeakable acts of sexual depravity performed on me, but to this day I have no memory of what took place. Having said that, I saw a film a few years later which was taken on that day and when I look back and remember that film and what was done to me it still makes me nauseous and angry.

I later found out that there was a drug in the hanky which made me easier to handle. I slowly came to myself. My body ached from head to foot. I became aware of my surroundings. Nikki and Tracey were cuddling me and I realized that we were no longer in the "playroom" but a bedroom. I was lying on an old four-poster bed and on the ceiling was a painting and a very crude one at that. I came to my senses very quickly when I saw that none of us had any clothes on. My embarrassment turned to modesty but I realized there was nowhere I could hide my body from them. Nikki seemed to sense my feelings and took hold of my hand. She told me not to worry, that no one else could see us. I was later to find out, as were all the others, there was nowhere in that house that was free from prying eyes or listening ears.

Nikki and Tracey helped me to dress. Nikki gave me a small bottle of about thirty pills (drugs). I was surprised there were so many. She told me that as long as I did as I was told I could have as many as I wanted along with all the money I could handle. But if I didn't . . . She left it hanging in mid-sentence. She didn't need to finish it off because I knew she meant that I would be punished, probably in a violent way.

Tracey told me that Nikki would be joining us in the taxi home, so we all made our way towards the stairs. My excitement at another taxi ride soon faded when I noticed a large bruise on Tracey's cheek. I asked her what had happened and she told me that the gladiator had punched her for being cheeky. He was called the gladiator because he liked to dress up as one, obviously, but he also liked to beat up children. I felt a burning anger, a madness if you like, that I had not felt before.

It wasn't the bruise on Tracey's face that angered me so much – that was just the tip of the iceberg – it was more the way I'd been treated all my life. Her bruise made me realize I had to do something but I was determined that I wouldn't land up with bruises like Tracey. I wanted revenge for me but it had to be done from a safe distance.

We were called a taxi and were taken home. The girls dropped me off around the corner from school and they went home. An hour later I went out to meet my mum as if nothing had happened.

Over the next year I was introduced to a way of life that was to become normal to me. This may be classed as a very sad and painful time, but to me it was perfectly normal because I knew no other.

You may ask what it is that makes me angry after all this time. It is not so much the sexual acts that were forced upon me. Those I can pretty much cope with now, although the memory of them still hurts from time to time. It is the fact that my childhood was stolen. The innocence that every child has was taken away from me. How can anybody give that back? Even if I could turn the clock back I would still be a child forced into being a man too early, a child of the '50s, with no other course to follow. I look around me today and find that the children and young people of the '90s are really no better off than I was. Forty years have passed and yet we are still sweeping things under the carpet. We have not moved forward an inch. You may think, this guy must be right unhappy, but you could not be more wrong. I am at long last moving forward, no longer trapped in the past even though the memories of those times still anger me.

4

My life settled into a pattern of sex, money and drugs.
The money and drugs were most important. Tracey and
I between us were earning over fifty pounds a week,
which was a lot of money in those days – it was like a
drug on its own – I craved more and more. It didn't
sink into my head that people were paying me to prosti-
tute my body. I liked the money and I spent it. I could
not understand why grown-ups would pay me so much
to perform acts of sex with them; I thought they were
quite mad. Tracey was right, the pain was gone. Sex no
longer made me sick. I had got used to it just as she
said I would. However, it would cause me a lot of
problems later in my life. Looking back now, I had
become able to sleep with anyone if the money was
right. By this time I was dependent on drugs which were
now no longer available for nothing. They had got me
hooked for free, but now I had to pay. I was paid for
my services with one hand and gave it back to them
with the other to pay for my drugs. The older I got the
more drugs I needed, the more money I had to earn.
Any money that I didn't use for drugs was stashed away
in my hide, hidden away from everybody. To be honest
I didn't really care how I came by the money as long
as I got it.

About six months after the first rape, I started to
cough a lot and was very short of breath. At the begin-

ning my parents thought it was just a chest infection – as our doctor had told them – but then I started coughing blood and losing a lot of weight. I was told then that it was asthma. It took me quite a number of years, in fact I was forty-one years old when I remembered the blood I had coughed up. You see, when I was a child my mind learnt the knack of blocking out painful things. I learnt later on that it was tuberculosis. I hadn't been told at the time because this was a disease that was greatly feared; most people didn't survive it.

It was decided that I would be sent to a private school on Clapham Common for children with learning difficulties. I had missed a lot of schooling so I had to catch up. I decided then and there that I didn't want to go. I didn't want to leave Tracey. My father discussed this with Tracey's parents. She'd had a lot of time off school due to her "activities" so her parents thought it a good idea if she went with me. They couldn't afford the fees so my father agreed to pay.

We were to be picked up every morning by a private coach and taken to this school. The first morning came. It was quite an event in our road and lots of people turned out to see us off. So off we went in our posh uniforms, with half the street waving goodbye to us. It was about half an hour's drive to the school. It was a lovely place. Lawns and flowerbeds surrounded it and we were open-mouthed at how clean it all was in amongst the decay and rot of London. It even smelled different, not of petrol and smoke but freshly cut grass. The classrooms were built in such a way that the sides could be opened up to give plenty of fresh air in the summer. Rest rooms were provided for us when our ailments got the better of us. Our lessons started early in the morning, around seven thirty, to allow for rest periods during the day, and finished at five in the evening. It was like a school and hospital in one. If we were unwell during the day they kept us overnight. Everything was done to make us comfortable, but in doing that they also made us aware that we were different from other children, so we did take a lot of liberties.

After we were shown around, we were ushered into the headmaster's office. We were both surprised to learn that we knew the headmaster, but we knew him as a doctor. He explained that the school was run as a hospital so that's why he was there. It seemed that wherever I went my reputation preceded me, for this was a man who was involved in the abuse of me and many other children and later he persuaded us to involve other children in school.

Looking back, I know it had nothing to do with my reputation. It was the fact that these people know and keep in touch with each other and pass children around like possessions. The impression the authorities give is that each paedophile ring is isolated from other rings. The opposite, I'm afraid, is true. Each ring has contact with others; it is very highly organized. Children are taken from one area and are usually transported to other parts of the country to avoid detection. There are people with power involved who force the lid to remain closed on the truth. Until the public start to ask questions loudly enough, this will continue to happen. I had seventeen years of involvement in this so you could say I am speaking from a position of knowledge. There is one question I keep asking myself: Why, if we value our children as much as we are supposed to, is there no national register for missing children? Or do we value cost more?

I became more involved in petty crime, stealing from local shops. A lot of the time I didn't steal for gain. It was as though I was trying to get caught, as if in my own way I was telling people all was not right with me. But nobody heard. In the words of Jesus, nobody had ears to listen. They were not looking for danger signs because they didn't know the danger signs existed. They didn't look closely enough. If they were guilty of anything it was that they didn't ask questions. Now I thank God that things are changing, slowly. People are at least aware now that children are being abused. But still not enough is being done. My wife can put into words both our feelings better than I can.

Take for example the case of a child, any child, anywhere in this country. The child has been abused, possibly by his/her father, stepfather, anybody in a position of trust to that child. The child decides that they can't go on like this and wants the abuse stopped. He decides to tell someone. Who? Mother? What will Mother's reaction be? Will the child be believed? The chances of being believed are fifty-fifty. In the case of this child the answer is yes. Then what? The mother confronts the abuser. He denies it. Doubt then begins to creep into the mother's mind as to the truth of it all. The abuse continues. The child then turns to another adult in a position of trust – a teacher. The teacher decides to act and tells the authorities. They question the child. The child already feeling hurt and confused by the situation then has to recount all instances of abuse whether he is ready to or not and the wheels of the system begin to turn. The authorities are faced with the denials of the abuser. Who is to be believed? The child who can't put into words the abuse he's suffered? Or, as he's now become known, the *alleged* abuser? The authorities cannot be sure that the *alleged* abuse isn't going to continue while the child remains in the house, so they obtain an order from the courts removing the child from home. The child by this time can't understand why all this is happening. All he wanted was the abuse to stop. Now he's being punished by being taken away from home. The authorities use this time that the child is out of the home to find out whether there are any physical signs of abuse by way of a medical examination, to gain a possible conviction. But the child doesn't want Daddy to go to prison. The child also doesn't want to be touched and looked at – that's just what Daddy did. The child on its own has no say, no right to say no. Hang on a minute. Aren't we teaching our children to do just that – say no? The child not only has a doctor looking at him and touching him but there are at least two other unknown people in the room, looking, staring, watching reactions.

This child is alone. These people were supposed to help the child and as far as society is concerned they are. But where is the child in all this? Left to come to terms with what's happened to him on his own. The desire for a conviction can cause the child so much pain, even though a member of the household has abused him. The child still feels affection, even loves the abuser, plus, he doesn't want to be the cause of the family break-up. Surely, what should be of paramount importance is the child, not that the law should have its pound of flesh. Why can't we put convictions onto the back burner for a while until the child is ready and able to cope with it? It must save long-term casualties. We adults understand the need for a quick conviction, but the child doesn't. When are the child's views and needs going to be taken into account?

There must be a better way to deal with child abuse than to split families up. We are storing up problems for the future. The abuser is locked up in prison. Some may say that's where he belongs. But is it? Many of these men never get any help and they come out of prison with as many hang-ups and problems as they had when they went in. The child is left probably in a children's home with no proper family life, no counselling to help him get over his problems and may well be abused again while he's there, so he grows up to be very bitter and with sexual and emotional problems of his own. What will happen in ten or fifteen years' time when the children of the families we are splitting up now grow up to be adults? We should be trying to keep these families together in the long term, get them working together, helping each other to overcome their problems and giving each and every individual involved counselling to come to terms with what's happened.

"All this is a necessary evil isn't it? If a child has been abused, then this is the only route we've got, so we have to take it," I hear you say. I believe that we have not reaped the "benefits" of these national policies yet. We have not seen yet to what extent these children have been affected once grown up. I believe that once it becomes known it will be too late for these children. We will have stolen their childhood and that can't be given back. The anger and bitterness they will feel will be directed at society and the problems that will bring, i.e. more abuse, more crime, and breakdown of relationships will be there for all to see.

This is only one side of the coin; the other side is the child whose parents have suspicion land on them for whatever reason and who *haven't* abused their child. This child has to go through exactly the same process as the abused child. He is medically examined and sometimes taken away from his family. Children such as these need special help because there is nothing at home that they have to be taken away from. It ruins children and breaks up marriages. That's why I believe there must be a better way of dealing with it.

As I have said earlier, when I was about eight years old, my mother and father noticed I kept getting erections. My mother made an appointment for me with a doctor at the local hospital. He examined me for about half an hour then told my mother that it was nothing to worry about, I had just started to develop early. I knew my mother wasn't convinced by that, but because he was the so-called expert she accepted what he told her. If she had questioned this diagnosis, she might have found out that this doctor was also a child abuser who remained one for another twenty-five years before someone did start asking questions and he was eventually struck off the medical register. At that time he was abusing me, but my mother didn't know any better.

Parents haven't got that excuse now – they are aware. The experts and the different authorities take action when abuse comes to light, but who takes action against them when things go wrong? Or are they immune? It is our job as parents to keep our eyes, minds and ears open to the kind of problems I faced as a child. Please don't go round with the "it can't happen to my children" syndrome, for it quite often does.

Some people may wonder why the signs I gave out were not picked up. The area I lived in and the way I was raised was a dog-eat-dog world. I was always told that if someone hit you with a small stick you hit them with a bigger one. An example of this was when I was little. My brother and I got into an argument over some wood we were messing around with. It ended up with him hitting me with this piece of wood and me returning the favour with a hammer. Both our heads were split open and we landed up in hospital having them sewn up. That, as far as my family were concerned, was normal behaviour – two brothers getting heated and striking out at each other. In fact it was me who had started the argument and me who had finished it.

The point I'm making is that we quite often saw adults reacting to each other in ways that ended in violence. I often witnessed my parents having some really violent arguments with each other, or they seemed that way to me. Or there were parties that would end in fights. My dad and my brothers were not shy in giving someone a whack on the nose or whatever else they could hit if they believed they deserved it. It was an accepted way of life. So for me to use violence – well, I was a chip off the old block, wasn't I? Violence was a part of my growing pains, as normal as having tea with cake. So when my behaviour did explode into violence it wasn't thought unusual. I was just like them, just like countless other people that lived near me. People aren't born violent. It is learnt behaviour from the example we are given and what we are taught.

In stark contrast, my wife's upbringing was completely different to mine. Her parents tried to break away from the "traditional working-class" way of life. Loud arguments were unheard of in their household. Their attitude to children was typically middle-class as was their attitude to behaviour. The image they tried to present was of perfect parents, so when I learned that my wife had been abused by her brother and many others for years, it shattered that image. I wanted to kill him. But the fact that he was her brother and the way she handled her abuse completely threw me. She still had contact with her brother and it was as though nothing had ever happened. Like me, she seemed to be looking for something in her life, but her behaviour was the complete opposite of mine. She didn't hate him. She didn't even resent her parents for not knowing about the abuse. I couldn't handle that. I'd never come across anyone who didn't hate their abuser. She didn't react violently. I wanted to but for her sake I couldn't. All I could do was to hate and hurt in my mind.

You see, my wife was brought up not to hurt people even if they hurt her, to be reasonable at all times. Everything was swept under the carpet. Bad things didn't happen in her family. They only happened in other families. The families who had bad things happen to them were classed as "those people". They were normally thought of as being deprived, socially and moneywise. My wife's violence was inwards, emotional, directed at herself, whereas mine was directed at other people and boy did they know it.

5

I had seen one side of abuse, but at the age of ten I was to see the other side – the dark, violent side that was not spoken of. I had been away from school for a few days as I was having a bad spell with my illness. But by Friday I was feeling better and decided to meet Tracey and tell her I would be back to school on Monday. It was to be a Friday I would not forget. Things were to happen that weekend that would change me yet again.

I met the school bus, but Tracey wasn't on it. I was told she had left early as she was not well. I was concerned – we often used the excuse of being unwell when we needed time off for meeting people. But she hadn't told me about any meeting this time. I turned to go home, then decided to go to the hide. On entering I saw Tracey. She was crying. Joan was there too, the girl from the TV star's house. I was angry that Tracey had shown Joan our secret place but I soon forgot my anger when I saw how upset she was. Joan was moaning like a wounded animal. I had never seen anyone so upset. Tracey asked me to help her to clean Joan up. As we started to undress her she shrank back, whimpering. She looked terrified of me, as though I would hurt her. I think it was more instinct than deliberate when I put my arm around her and kissed her on the cheek. I told her that I wouldn't hurt her and that I loved her. I told her to let us help her. She threw her arms around me, hugged me and just cried and cried. She took my face in her hands and said, "Gus, if I should disappear, tell someone." She made us both promise that we would. I'm thirty years late but now I'm telling someone.

Looking back I can remember Joan's perfect body, but that day as we helped her to undress, what I was looking at wasn't lovely at all. I couldn't believe what I saw and I recoiled in horror. Her back was a bloody mess as were her sides and stomach. Deep jagged scratches lined her back, the bone was visible in quite a few places and it was difficult to see where one gouge ended and another began. It looked as though forks had been stuck in her and raked through the flesh. She was completely ripped open. I cried out in shock or anger, I still don't know which. Joan was more concerned for me than she was for herself. She hugged me and told me that it looked worse than it was. I asked her what kind of person would do something like this. Her reply still shocks and angers me to this day. "It was our lovely headmaster."

I asked her what had happened. The full story I will not recount because of its horror. Let's just say that there were dogs involved, more than one I might add. I'll leave the rest to your imagination. Even to my hardened mind I honestly couldn't believe that a man could be so cruel and twisted as to do such a wicked thing to a young girl.

We cleaned her up as best we could with what little we had in the hide. She told me she was going to report him to the police. She had told him this also but he had just laughed. Tracey begged her not to say anything.

We both knew what would happen if she did, as did Joan. She was past caring though by this time. She said she had to let someone know what was going on and made me promise again to tell if she disappeared. I laughed and told her she'd be O.K. Joan just smiled. She gave us both a kiss as we helped her out of the hide. As she walked away she turned and said, "Don't forget me, Angus." She was never seen again.

Joan was put down as a runaway. I know she didn't run away and I came to know many more like Joan. Of those who disappeared or turned up dead, all had told at least one person that they were going to talk. The coincidence seems too great as far as I'm concerned. If I'm unlucky, sometimes I see her in my dreams but not as the lovely young girl. The good thing is those dreams don't come too often.

I left the school soon after and was sent off to boarding school. My condition was getting worse and my parents had heard of a new school that was having a lot of success, so it was decided, I think as a last resort, to give it a try.

I took my leave of London at the age of ten and a half and went down to the Surrey countryside. What a change! I had never seen so much grass, trees and animals. There was a deer park next door to the school and the deer were tame enough to eat out of your hand. It was so peaceful, I felt better as soon as I got there. But I missed my family and Tracey and, believe it or not, I missed the other side of my life too. I missed the rewards and the drugs world. I missed the excitement. I missed being the centre of attention and also I missed the sex.

But not for long. Tracey sent me parcels of drugs after a short while and Gino was to visit me on a number of occasions. He would take me to a cottage for "work", where I would also get more drugs. I was to meet another girl, Carol, who was thirteen. She was to become not only my lover but a lifelong friend. I introduced her to the sex ring by taking her along to the cottage. Each child involved would be encouraged to get other children to take part. In doing so there would be extra drugs and because they were new to it they would get all the attention and we would be left alone for a time. Carol became as involved as me and a drug user.

I was also to lose another friend, Jan. She died at the age of eleven of tuberculosis. She was a lovely girl and the first one to speak to me about Jesus, though at the time I thought she had a screw loose because of her illness. She wasn't frightened of death at all, in fact she looked on it more as going home. She had the habit of creeping into my bed at night for company as we both missed our families and she always felt cold. Then early in the morning she would creep back into her own bed. It was our little secret.

. She crept in one night, telling me she was really tired. She cuddled into me and we both fell asleep. I awoke the following morning feeling very scared and freezing cold. Jan was still cuddled into me but she was dead. She'd died in her sleep. I was punished when we were found and thrown into a room and left there all that day.

I became very ill quite soon afterwards. Whether it was the shock or not, I don't know, but I collapsed and became unconscious. How long I was in this state I can't tell, but I do know it was quite some time. I was to have my first meeting then with the one I had declared war on at the age of seven. I was tired and in pain and just wanted to sleep and never wake up. That was when God spoke to me. I have no doubt that it was God. He told me that my time was not up, that I would get better and that I had work to do for Him. I did wake up and I did get better. I went from strength to strength, but the words He had spoken with such care and love became a faded memory. I was still at war with God, still believing He was to blame. I would continue to blame Him for many years to come. It didn't occur to me that I could be so wrong.

After spending about eighteen months at the school I was sent home, back to London, back to "work". My life settled back into the same pattern with the exception of two vital changes. Gino noticed that my body was fully developed. He also found out that Tracey and I were sexually involved, so he sent me to the young wife of a famous man and I supplied her with my services. She paid me five pounds. I later found out that she had paid a boy called Tony twenty-five pounds, a lot of money to me. So I decided to get my own clients and do away with the middle man, which is what I did and it worked.

I continued in this line of work for fourteen years. They had trained me well. I could have clients one after the other for days on end yet I didn't seem to tire like other people.

The other change was that now relatives began abusing me. This was to close the door on any chance I had of my abuse coming to light. You see, even though I was involved in a porn ring, my family life and home were separate. Any trust that was left between my family and me was now broken. Now it wasn't only happening with people I didn't know, it was happening with people I loved. I was beginning to think and was in fact told by one of my brothers that what he was doing was perfectly normal. I had no reason to doubt him. It must have been normal; everybody was doing it. I didn't tell him about the other people I was involved with. I wanted to keep the money and rewards for myself and I wasn't going to share them with anyone.

There was now me, Tracey and Carol who'd come back to London with me. We were the gang of three. It was us against them. We guarded our world and didn't let anyone else in.

Nothing much changed in my life. Wealthy people paid well for my services and there were others who just gave rewards. They were the worst. They were met mainly at parties the rich and powerful attended. There, unspeakable acts took place. I could write a thousand pages about all the things that went on but it would be one horror after another. I feel there is no need for that. I could also write a new version of *Who's Who* including all the people I met, but what would be the point in that? It would prove nothing.

I was becoming more involved in bigger crimes. As the gang of three we started to break into chemist shops where we would head for what used to be called the "A" list drug cabinet or little black box as it was known. I would steal a motorbike and ride pillion with a sledgehammer. Tracey would wait about a mile away with a large shopping trolley. Carol would pull up outside the chemist's and I would jump off, swinging my sledgehammer as I went. Normally I would aim at the door as it broke more easily. Once inside, my sledgehammer would go to work on the drug cabinet. I'd pick it up, get back on the bike and away. Most times it could be done in less than a minute though there was always a chance of getting caught. Enter Tracey with the shopping trolley. We would meet her somewhere quiet and tip the contents of the cabinet into her trolley. She would make her way back to the hide and we'd dump the bike and meet her there. If the shop didn't have an alarm or a flat above it we could take our time and there was no need for the sledgehammer. We preferred these shops because we could take more and there was less chance of getting caught. Sledgehammers were OK but they were a little too noisy.

Things didn't always go as planned. There was one chemist we did and, as I had the box in my arms I didn't have time to hold on before Carol roared away and I found myself sitting in the road with a sore backside and pills everywhere. I felt a tap on my shoulder. Looking up I saw a CID sergeant that I knew.

"Well, Angus, what's all this about?"

I looked at him with my mouth wide open. "Well, Sarge, it was like this. I was walking along minding my own business and, well, this box just hit me."

He laughed and was just about to say something to me when we heard the roar of a motorbike. I jumped up and fast. It was Carol. I didn't know what she was going to do but I thought I'd get out of the way just in case. We both jumped apart as she shot between us, leg outstretched to kick the copper. She must've got confused because I landed up back on my knees again not knowing where to rub first – my backside or groin –

both were pretty painful. The policeman was hopping around holding his foot. Carol had just run over his toe and it sounded as though she'd broken it. She had jumped the pavement and landed in a flowerbed. I thought she'd completely flipped. She was rolling around on the ground in hysterics. Every time she looked at us she collapsed again. To finish my little tale, Tracey came walking along as if she was out shopping. I took one look at her and also fell about laughing.

This episode did have a good ending, luckily for us. The friendly little policeman not only had a sense of humour, but, like a lot of his colleagues was bent, on the take. So we didn't get arrested. We dealt with him for quite a number of years until we turned the tables on him and persuaded him to leave the force.

The gang of three carried on as before; we were still tops. How long we were to remain there we were soon to find out.

Carol's parents decided to move north because of her father's job. Carol was allowed to stay behind. We had a great party after they left. If they had come back there would've been hell to pay. There we were, dancing around the room, Carol wearing nothing but a short nightie and Tracey and I naked. We were all stoned out of our minds and it seemed that whatever we did or touched turned to gold. We had a three-bedroomed detached house all to ourselves – not bad for Tracey and Carol, fifteen and sixteen respectively and me coming up for fourteen. But everything has its price, and we were about to pay ours.

Sue arrived at the house. (Her real name is not being used so her memory can be protected.) Her mum and stepdad were very wealthy people with a title but her stepfather had been abusing her since she was ten years old. (She was sixteen now.) We had met four years previously and had remained good friends. So there we were, all having a good time when Tracey, for no reason, burst into tears. I was shocked. I really didn't know what was wrong. Sue took me into the kitchen and told me to stay there. She came back about half an hour later and told me to go and have a chat with Tracey. I asked her how she was and she said, "Apart from being pregnant, she's fine." My mouth fell open.

"How did that happen?"

"Well," said Sue and sarcastically began to explain how babies were conceived.

"OK, OK, Sue. I mean she's not old enough is she?" I really couldn't understand this.

Sue assured me. "Not only is she old enough, but so are you!"

I felt dazed, I wasn't quite with it anyway, being stoned, but this really smacked me in the chops. When I came to myself I thought, Oh, no, how do I explain this to Mummy and Daddy? This will really put the cat among the pigeons. I'd been in trouble so many times, but this would be like an A bomb to them. I wasn't even fourteen and I was already a prospective father.

I went in to Tracey. She was still upset. Then she was saying sorry and I was saying sorry to her, then we just hugged each other. Carol and Sue came in later and we all sat down. We talked about what we were going to do. They talked and for once I listened. Half the time I didn't know what they were talking about. The word abortion was mentioned and it was agreed she should have one. Sue said she would phone a lady in Chelsea who was a friend of her mother's and it would cost fifty pounds. She told me not to worry as she'd had one herself when she was twelve. She assured us that it would all be over in a couple of hours. I wasn't even sure what she was speaking about, so I left them to arrange it all.

The woman arrived a few hours later. She took Tracey out to the kitchen. She was gone about half an hour, then she was back. I gave her the fifty pounds and she was gone. For a morning I was a dad, even if I wasn't quite sure what had gone on, I still felt something – a sense of loss, I suppose.

Carol called me into the kitchen. There on the table was a perfect little person. It looked so lovely, like a rose that had started to bloom. The promise of such loveliness to come, killed off before it had a chance.

Sue started to wrap the body up. I ran over and told her I would do it. So I wrapped up my child, went out into the garden and buried it along with a little piece of me. I swore I would never again allow that to happen. I went back into the house. Carol and Sue told me Tracey was upstairs asleep and not to disturb her. I would like to say I cried or showed my feelings about my child, but I didn't. I was past feeling love or hurt about anything. Pain didn't register any more – I'd been hurt too many times. Now I'm different. I can grieve for lots of things and I do grieve for that child.

Tracey slept for a couple of hours. She woke up screaming! We ran upstairs. She was in agony and there was so much blood. Sue phoned the woman who had come earlier to ask for help. She told Sue that she wouldn't come and to take her to hospital.

We got Tracey dressed and into Sue's car. We drove her to the hospital and by the time we arrived she was unconscious. We took her to casualty. They wanted to know her name and everything about her. We couldn't tell them anything because abortion was illegal then and we thought we'd go to prison. We told them she'd collapsed outside on the pavement. They thanked us and we left.

Later that night Sue phoned the hospital telling them she was Tracey's sister only to be told that she had died without regaining consciousness. After nearly seven years together we didn't get the chance to say goodbye.

I reacted as I always had done. I just locked away the hurt and grief. You see it hadn't happened to me. It was always someone else that these bad things happened to. I suppose it was the only way I could cope with it at the time. I was told afterwards that she'd died of some kind of flu. I knew differently. Families then didn't want anyone to know when their daughters became pregnant let alone if they had an abortion. The social stigma surrounding unmarried mothers was appalling, so parents either hid their daughters away until the birth or they paid for a back-street abortion and kept it quiet.

6

After the death of Tracey, my life didn't change. It went on as before. I had become so cold and unfeeling, it was as if she had never been. I had given up on the human race long before the death of Tracey. Her death to me then was just the loss of a money-making object that I had to find a replacement for. But later, her death was to come back and haunt me for years. Then I would have to pay a huge price.

I had to avenge Tracey, not for me, but in the world I lived in; if I let her death go unpunished, I would lose face and that would be taken as a sign of weakness. I would then be taken advantage of. So the abortionist had to pay. Sue decided to have a chat with a man she knew in government circles, and I talked to the wife of a law enforcement officer.

Her house was gutted by fire – it was put down to a gas leak – but we knew better. She was arrested very soon afterwards for drug offences and received a small prison term. After leaving prison she went to live in France. Sue later told me the woman had died. I didn't ask how or when. I wasn't really interested. As far as I was concerned Tracey had been avenged and I had shown people not to mess with me.

I was slowly moving out of prostitution with men as I became more in demand by women. We were now into the swinging sixties and I had reached my teenage years – free love, free drugs, make love not war. I agreed with all that as long as they paid and paid well. You see, while the rest of my generation was protesting for peace, I was involved in a war, the war of the streets where it was dog eat dog and I was determined not to be the bone.

I had been trained well in how to use my body, but I hadn't been taught how to use my brain. I was going to have to learn fast if I wanted to survive. Over the next five or six years, I learned how to lie. I learned how to manipulate the powerful people I was involved with. I didn't believe that I was selling my body. I never felt dirty or used. As far as I was concerned it was me who was using them. I enjoyed the money and the drugs. The ladies – well they were an added perk. I didn't realize the trouble I was storing up for myself in later years.

I was now beginning to diversify. I had been involved with these people now for nine years and as in any "business" you get promoted. I thought I was in control of the direction in which my life was going. I wanted to make more money so, as I see now, was led into transporting drugs. Most times Sue would go with me as a decoy. She was also well known, so nine out of ten times nobody bothered us. Sometimes we very nearly lost our "cargo", not to the police but to rival gangs who were always on the lookout for easy pickings. If we went back empty-handed we would more than likely lose some of our body parts and I was quite fond of all of mine.

Sue and I this particular time had to take a parcel of dope across London. I was going to use one of my father's vans but Sue said that would be too risky as the Old Bill were becoming more aware of drugs, which was not surprising as many off-duty policemen were using drugs themselves. A lot of our deals were with policemen but there were a lot of straight police around as well so we had to be careful.

We decided on public transport eventually as there was safety in numbers, so we got on the tube. We were soon aware of three young men following us. I told Sue to take the parcel and go to the other side of the train as though she was going to get off. She did as I said and made out she was getting off. Just before the doors closed she screamed and fell forward and the men thinking she'd fainted became careless. They lunged forward to catch her. She wriggled away and fell onto the platform. At the same time I attacked them from behind, slashing two of them across the back of neck. The third turned and as he did so I caught him straight across the face. Just in time I managed to dive through the doors before they closed behind me. I helped Sue up and and we ran along the platform, home and dry.

We made our way to the ladies toilets – after all that work we needed some gear. Sue told me that a good friend had given her some really nice coke and did I want some. I told her I wasn't into coke and that I had some speed. She snorked a line and fell over. She was dead before she hit the floor. I felt her pulse to make sure. I wasn't mistaken.

I took the parcel, left the toilet and just walked away. Fourteen years old and I just walked away; there was nothing I could do for her. This is not a good day, I thought. You see, when somebody died like that you couldn't stop and think about it. I didn't want anyone seeing me. I had to get out of there quickly, not because I was frightened, but because I had a parcel of drugs that was worth a lot of money. All a drug addict thinks about is his fix; nothing else concerns him at all. His mother can die and if she's got money on her at the time, he will take it so he can get his next fix. Morals, fear, concern for others are not part of a drug addict's life.

I made my way to Carol's, making sure I had not been seen. Then it hit me. It needn't be a bad day after all. I decided to tell everybody concerned that Sue had the parcel and I'd had to leave it. Nice one, I thought. I've made five hundred pounds. Thank you, Sue, not a bad day's work.

It wasn't hard to work out that somebody somewhere had wanted Sue out of the way. She never used street pushers. She didn't have to, she was rich. Street pushers tamper with gear to expand their profits. The people she obtained her drugs from didn't need to do that, so any tampering with it would have been intentional. Just another dead junkie; that's what the world would say. Eighteen years old – what a life!

It was just after this that Carol took her leave of me. She was working in a club, dancing, among other things, and a nice wealthy older man took quite a shine to her. They married and although she was to become a widow quite soon, she was set up for life. She didn't go back to her old life except for one small slip.

I was now alone for the first time in my life. Carol was married and gone, Tracey and Sue were dead. There were still people involved in child porn. I was still involved in prostitution, having grown too old to be of any use in child porn, but I had no one close to me any more.

I met my first wife Anne at a bus stop at the age of seventeen. We got talking and eventually started courting. It wasn't a smooth-running courtship by any stretch of the imagination. My family didn't like her and her family didn't like me, and me – well by now I didn't like me much either. I needed someone in my life that was clean, free from drugs and crime. I was moving in an ever deceasing circle of drug addicts and I needed a "front" to make me look respectable. I also needed a cover for my criminal activities. The police were getting too close for comfort and I had to have space, room to manoeuvre. Anne and married life were to give me that; they were to give me the independence I needed. At least, I thought, it would get my parents off my back and possibly a home of my own. Anne, like my mother and father, thought I had a drink problem and it gave me a good cover for my drug taking. To have a drink problem was socially acceptable but to take drugs, man, that was not on. It was to be kept hidden and quiet at all costs.

I had been courting Anne for about three months when Carol came to see me. She said Gino had visited her. He and other people wanted her back to use her to "break in" young boys. They were threatening to tell her husband about her past. He knew a little bit but not the complete horror of what she'd been involved in and, well, I don't suppose he would've been over the moon if he found out. Gino had made her promise to meet him the following day and she really didn't want to go as she knew what would happen. I asked her where she had to meet him. She told me of a houseboat in Chelsea that he had the use of. I told her to go and she asked what I was going to do. I told her to wait and see. Immediately I thought I would use the situation to settle a few old scores. I was going to pay him back for the pain he'd caused me all those years.

I was seventeen years old but I was like an animal. I was angry and had been for years but I'd never had the chance or the courage to have a go at Gino and the others openly. I had always done it anonymously. Now I didn't care. I wanted them to know it was me and I was going to take this opportunity with both hands. Although I had wanted revenge for a long time, they'd had such a hold over me that I'd never felt it possible. There were always too many people around. Now I knew Gino would be on his own I thought this would probably be my only chance. I had become as bad as them. I'd always seen them as the abusers and I was the victim. Now I wanted to become the abuser. I wanted to terrify this man the way he had terrified me and let him know that enough was enough. He had led me into a lifestyle of addiction. I wasn't only addicted to drugs but by now I was also addicted to sex. I still felt trapped and the only way I felt I could break away from it all was to get rid of Gino.

I managed to get hold of a van after a bit of blackmail. I also obtained a pump-action shotgun, a can of petrol and a baseball bat. I was all set – I was going to make his day.

Carol and I made our way to Chelsea the following day. We had agreed, once he was naked, Carol would make an excuse, go up onto the deck and wave to let me know. Then I would make my move. Men don't always fight well when they are naked so I would be at an advantage, or at least that's what I told myself. All I had to do was wait for Carol.

I waited. What the heck was keeping her? She'd been in there over half an hour. Bloody women, I thought, can't get anything right. My mind then flashed back to Tracey, Sue and all the other girls I had known who hadn't made it. For a moment I was really sure I felt the start of a tear. Bloody fool, I thought, Gino's for me. I had waited with great patience for over ten years. He was mine all mine. My thoughts were interrupted by Carol at long last appearing on deck. She looked very flustered. I got out of my van with my baseball bat, petrol and shotgun and made my way over to the houseboat.

Even when I got in there I had every intention of killing him. He was lying on the couch. On the table next to him were some lines of cocaine, so I knew he was stoned. He realized what I was going to do when I picked up the petrol can and he began to whimper. Carol realized too and ran over to stand between Gino and me.

"No, Gus, don't kill him."

At that moment I was in such a rage all I could feel was my hatred for this person. I picked up the shotgun and aimed it at Carol.

"Get out of my way or you go too."

She refused to move. "Look," she said, "he's not worth it."

"Let me shoot him," I insisted.

"No." By this time she was pleading. "I'm married now. I've got a new life. If you do this they'll not only put you away for life, they'll put me away too."

"How do you work that one out?" I said.

"I'M HERE, YOU DODO," she screamed. "Don't ruin my life. Look at him. He won't hurt either of us

70

now. This is the man who has held us in fear for years. He's a snivelling wreck."

I looked at him. She was right. He was nothing but a quivering lump of jelly. I put the gun down. "OK, but I'm not letting him get away scot-free."

I asked Gino where the money was. He tried to tell me that there wasn't any. I picked up the gun and levelled it at him. At the same time Carol picked up the box of matches.

He screamed, "OK, all right, I'll get it. It's under the couch." He lifted up the seat.

"Very slowly, Gino, we don't want any accidents do we?" I said. By this time my rage had subsided somewhat, but I didn't want him to know that. I wanted him to think I was crazy.

He lifted out a black case and laid it on the floor. I told him to push it over to Carol. She opened it – it was full to the brim with money. We counted it later and it came to just over five thousand pounds.

I knew there was a secret room on that boat. In it was a hidden camera used for filming orgies. I also knew he kept quite a few photos and documents in there too. I told Carol to go and get them and load them into the back of the van. He started to tell me I must not take them and I swung the gun round and pointed it right at him. He screamed and threw himself down on the floor with his head in his hands, telling me to take what I wanted. I assured him I was going to do just that. Carol came back and told me she'd got everything.

"What about him?" she said.

I pointed to some rope lying in the corner and she went over to it and proceeded to tie Gino up. She was as disgusted as I was at this sorry excuse for a man. When she was finished, she told him never to contact her again or the stuff we had stolen would be made public. He knew she meant it as her husband was a man of wealth and influence.

Gino didn't give us any trouble after that. In fact I only saw him occasionally when I delivered gear to him. I often wanted to finish off the job I'd started but to be honest part of me was happy enough with the result I'd already got. I felt I now was in a bargaining position. I had removed him as the controller of my life. But I didn't realize at the time that there would be others who would take his place and these people had a lot more power than Gino ever had.

I became more and more involved in violent crime, armed robberies, burglaries and debt collecting. If people didn't want to pay then my trusty baseball bat or petrol can soon changed their minds.

I had come a long way from the innocent little seven-year-old who was led to the slaughter like a lamb. When I look back now I am shocked at what I had become. I used and abused people as if they were there for my personal use and to hell with their feelings. I had none and I thought that everyone else who did were just wimps. They were not important – only my survival mattered.

As I said, I was courting Anne. She was so different to me. I thought it was quite normal for us to make love, but Anne had other ideas. She made it plain she did not sleep with boys and she was saving herself for her husband. To keep the peace I went along with it. I was sleeping with four or five women a week, so I wasn't really concerned. I soon learned that in the real world, when a nice girl said no she really meant no, but you still had to try for that was part of the courting. Eventually after a time she would give in. I found all this very confusing to say the least. So did Anne apparently.

As you must know by now I wasn't a normal boy. I really knew about love-making. I had been taught from the age of nine to please women in bed, so when she did give me an inch she found me taking a yard. It caused a lot of rows between us. She wanted to know how I knew so much. I had no answer.

We had a big argument one time when she suspected I was not only seeing other girls but sleeping with them. My mother had a row with Anne about keeping me out till the early hours of the morning. She had said to my mum, "Well, I don't know where he gets to because he leaves me around ten." This made her even more suspicious about other women and it resulted in a blazing row. I used this as a good excuse to go to sea in the merchant navy. This fitted in well with my plans as I was very heavily into drugs and money trafficking.

I took my leave of Anne and my family and made my way to Port Talbot in Wales to join my first ship. I already had a deal lined up before I went. I had to pay some money to a lady in Marseilles who would give me a packet containing heroin. Next stop Holland. There I bought some more heroin and when I got back home I made a very big profit.

I quite enjoyed my short time in the navy. For the first time in my life I was on my own, away from my family and Anne. Nobody knew me. I could decide what I did and how I did it and I didn't have to give account of myself to anyone except the captain and the head deckhand of course. The work wasn't hard and for a short time I was happy. But then as always my past caught up with me.

I shouldn't have been surprised because it had been so easy for me to go to sea. My brother had been in the merchant navy and he'd had to go to cadet school. But I just went to see a guy in the City on the Monday, he made a phone call and I joined my first ship a few days later. This man was a member of the sex ring who passed me over to the woman in Port Talbot. It was like a continuous conveyer belt and I felt I had no way of getting off.

My time in the navy was short-lived. I was involved in an incident in France where a friend of mine was set upon on leaving a restaurant and nearly beaten to death. As they left him his attackers told him to return the papers etc. he had stolen. They addressed him as Angus. Boy, was I glad I'd stayed on board that night.

It was too dangerous to stay where I was, so when we docked in Leith in Scotland, I decided to jump ship. I stole some money and went to stay with my sister in Dundee, which is about forty miles from Leith. I needed time to think, to work out my next move. I had a lot of money and drugs put to one side but there were some very powerful people after my blood.

I had to work out a plan or I would go missing like so many before me. I decided to split up all the photos, films and other papers I had. I made copies of a lot of them and sent them to important people who were, and in some cases still are, involved in child porn. I let it be known that I had also sent copies to people in the media.

The outcome was that they told me if I toed the line

I would be left alone. If I didn't, then they wouldn't touch me but my family. Obviously I wasn't happy with that but there wasn't an awful lot I could do about it.

Time went on. I'd rejoined my wife-to-be and we were still at loggerheads. I'd spent a short spell in Ashford remand centre on charges of grievous bodily harm and criminal damage. Needless to say I was just as violent in there as I was on the outside and became involved in a riot. I was only there for two weeks.

Things as usual weren't going very well, so I decide to try for a career in the army as I had good training for it!! It was to be a very bad mistake. I detested the life. I don't recall much about it but I do remember that I tried my hardest to get out again and that I was worse when I came out than when I went in. So the army and I parted company. I was told I was not suitable and not required.

So off I went, back to London and my real career in drugs and crime. I knew I was suited to that. Anne and I patched up our differences and decided to get married. Everyone was taken aback by our sudden announcement. They all thought she was pregnant. We had a huge wedding with hundreds of guests. The north of Scotland was the destination of our honeymoon. We had typical north-of-the-border weather – we were snowed in. Not that we noticed. We only left our hotel room once and that was to go out for some beer.

Perhaps this was going to be the start of a new life for me. Maybe I could at last lead a normal life. But how? I wasn't sure if I could. I didn't know how to behave the way "normal" people did. Perhaps if people would stop harassing me, I thought, I might get somewhere. Maybe.

7

As a married man at the age of twenty, I enjoyed my new found freedom to start with. I didn't have to make excuses for staying out late or explain where I had been. I had removed my mother, father and the rest of my family from the scene. I no longer had to worry about them. I did have a wife, though, who asked questions, but she was only one person. I had exchanged a dozen people for one.

I had to find time for my criminal activities and give reasons to Anne for my absences from home. The answer to my problem came not from me but from Anne. She gave me the excuses I needed.

She was moaning about my family. She said my brothers and I spent too much time in the pub and working in my father's transport business. It was the perfect answer. I played my family against my wife and vice versa. If I spent a night or two away from home my brothers covered for me. I was the young stud, the hard drinking, hard living young man – normal. They told my wife I was working. She was the nagging wife at home as far as they were concerned and they all had one just the same at home. She didn't get much change from my brothers' wives either. When she spoke to them about it their response was – well, men were like that. She should enjoy her own life and just ignore the bad bits. But she wasn't happy with the way things were and the harder she tried to change things the more unhappy she became.

Me, I was perfectly happy. As long as I acted like other married men, or most of them, things were OK for me. The thing was, I had terrible problems. I often wonder what excuses other men gave. Just that, well, that's how men are? But are we really like that? I don't think so. We men are not born to be so uncaring; we just allow ourselves to become that way so that other men will think how manly we are. Are we that vain? I think a lot of us are. I know I used to be. Am I now? I'll let you be the judge of that.

My violence and drug addiction landed me in more trouble before I was married. Anne thought it was a one-off thing that happened because of an argument we'd had. She could not have been more wrong. I was on a come-down. I hadn't had my fix so I was depressed, feeling sick, angry and in pain. A guy I didn't like much landed up being beaten with a walking stick. I was arrested and remanded to Ashford for two weeks for reports. This was my first taste of prison.

I was bundled into a prison van. It was like a large delivery lorry only it was divided up into approximately twelve little boxes which were roughly two feet wide by about two feet long. Each box or "cell" had a small square window high up on the side of the van. There was enough room to sit bolt upright but not enough to adjust your position. So there I was, handcuffed and sitting in this "sweat box" on my way to prison.

We arrived at the prison reception where I was stripped of my clothes and poked and prodded by a prison officer. He was talking, as I thought, to a boy standing next to me and it wasn't until he poked me in the chest that I realized he was speaking to me.

"I'm talking to you, boy. Are you in for reports to see if you've any loose screws?"

"I didn't know you were talking to me. You were looking at the boy next to me," I said. "Secondly, if I'm mad then you must come a close second. Thirdly, don't poke me."

He replied, "One, I wasn't looking at the boy next to you, I've got a bit of a squint."

I laughed and made a sarcastic comment. As soon as I opened my mouth I'd pressed my self-destruct button. Part of me wanted to make people think I was crazy, because if they did they stayed away – eventually. I wanted nothing but to be left alone, but my words and actions got me the complete opposite. I was dragged away and found myself with no clothes in another little cell. This one had cloth pads all over the walls and ceiling – even the door was covered. I was in my first but not last padded cell.

An eye spoke to me through a little hole. "We'll get you in the morning."

I'd seen it all now – a speaking eye. Aaargh. With all the drugs I was taking I couldn't take anything seriously. Looking back I think I must've been going crazy. My mind was going completely. So I had a tab of acid to help get my mind together and settled down to wait for morning to come. They had taken all of my clothes, poked and prodded me for drugs or whatever else they were looking for yet ignored the small plaster on my finger. I had enough dope to last me a day or two. I could also sell a few tabs in exchange for other drugs. I decided this place wasn't too bad.

With my LSD, the night soon gave way to morning. The eye was speaking to me again, telling me to move away from the door. Now this was hard because I didn't even know where the door was. I wondered, would the floor open up and swallow me, or perhaps the ceiling would open and a hand reach down and grab me for breakfast. But no, the wall opened, and there stood my officer from the night before. He informed me that I had been placed on report for insulting behaviour. I apologized to his eye for any offence I had caused it. He was not amused at this either and slung me a shirt and a pair of trousers and told me to follow him for breakfast. Even when I knew it would make me more enemies than I already had I didn't back down. In my drug-induced state I just didn't care.

They had taken everything away from me I could use as a weapon, yet they handed me a metal tray with three compartments – a first-class weapon. When a boy came up to me and said he was going to get me later, I said, "How about now, mug?" and hit him with the tray. He dropped like a stone. The "screws" came rushing in and I received quite a beating which landed up as a full-scale riot.

I spent another night in my little padded cell dressed in what's known as a Gary Glitter suit – a pair of shorts and top with handcuffs attached to the waist to prevent me from moving my hands and straps around the ankles, which meant that I could only take very small steps when walking.

The next day I was moved to the hospital wing where I spent the next two weeks. There I saw a doctor for all of ten minutes.

I went back to court and was given a twelve months'

conditional discharge and ordered to pay costs of three pounds, twenty-five pence.

You see it paid to have friends in high places. I had been visited in prison by a man who worked in the Home Office. He assured me that as long as I said nothing about my other activities everything would be fine. I told him I would do what he wanted but I needed some smokes and some gear. He told me my needs would be met. He even told me what would happen when I went to court. He was right. Everything happened as he said it would. As long as I kept my mouth shut things would be OK.

Anne thought it was all a silly misunderstanding, a one-off thing. But as married life continued she saw another side of me, a side my family never saw, a dark side – the bursts of rage, the coldness, the criminal side of me. I would disappear for days at a time and reappear without an explanation. She was desperately trying to make sense of it all and finding it impossible.

Then came the bust-up with my family. I was stealing from the family business. Not that I needed the money, I didn't. But I was spending more money than I legitimately had and I needed an explanation for my wife and family as to where it was coming from. So I gave them an answer. When they found out there was an almighty row and I left the business.

Now I was free of my family. This was better for me because I didn't have to explain where my money came from and I also had a lot more time to myself. I gave the excuse to Anne that I wanted to get on in the world and do well, so I got a job as a lorry driver which enabled me to spend longer hours away from home. Anne accepted this and the arguments diminished.

I was slipping in and out of the country all the time, short one- or two-day trips, taking money out and drugs back. I would like to say it was hard to escape detection, but it wasn't; it was really quite easy. Some couriers are meant to get caught and when they were stopped, I slipped through behind them. This was only one way into the country; there were many others. As I said before, there were always rival gangs trying to elbow their way in and steal the merchandise. There were plenty of stabbings and shootings and quite a few were killed. I was lucky. I've been stabbed and shot at but I always managed to get away.

But this lifestyle was telling on me. I was becoming very depressed, nervous and even more violent in my private life. I very nearly choked Anne during an argument one night in which she flushed my last bit of heroin down the toilet. When told by Anne, my family, not wanting to accept that I was on drugs put it down to my drinking and said I needed a rest, so Anne wasn't believed. They blamed her and said she was putting too much pressure on me. She couldn't win. My family told her that if I were to become a dad it might change me and I might settle down.

So Anne decided to give it a try – after all what did she have to lose? Only her marriage.

Anne had seen my violence inside our marriage and heard many times of my violence on the streets, but all she was told was that it was only because I was a bit wild. She was slowly becoming terrified of me. I had tried to kill her, yet she was given no help. Even when she did complain to the doctor and both our families about my constant demands for sex, she was told that her duty as a wife was to see to my needs. Even if she didn't want sex, she was told, she had to say yes. She didn't have the right to say no; after all she was my wife, wasn't she? She was just as much a victim as I was. I abused her just as much as I had been abused. How much has changed today? Do women have more rights? Ask men and their answer is a definite yes, ask women the same question and you'll get a very different answer.

I suppose it's because I've been raped and abused so badly myself that I can stand now where women stand and see things from their point of view. Plus, in counselling I have come to terms with what I suffered and also what I have done to others.

My drug addiction was taking such a hold of me I began to find it very hard to hold down a regular job. The wages I was being paid weren't even enough to support my wife let alone an ever increasing drug habit. So I used to take unofficial time off to earn more money. I began to find that I couldn't concentrate for very long so I was forever forgetting what I was supposed to be doing. This would result in my employer pulling me to one side for not completing my work. I would fly into a rage. As far as I was concerned I had completed, so I couldn't understand why people were having digs at me all the time.

Even now I have this problem with my memory. I have since found out from my medical records that I had seen quite a few doctors who said I had problems with my memory and that I had a personality disorder. Yet none of them realized I was a heroin addict. The two doctors I did confide in about my addiction told me not to tell anyone for the sake of my family. A drink problem is one thing, they said. That is acceptable, but not drugs. The family would never live that down, would they? Today it is not much different. I can sympathize with people who are HIV Positive. They too are treated like social lepers.

To add to all these problems, my wife announced she was pregnant. My first reaction was to be very happy, but inside I was terrified. How could I be a father? How could I support a child, and would the people I was involved with try to get my child as they had got me? I was really in despair and I didn't know what to do.

8

Thinking back, this was the worst possible time to become a father. Looking at what I went through in my life I don't think any time was the "right" time. Putting everything else aside, my drug-taking was expanding. I was starting to take LSD (acid) and with all the other problems I was having this was just about the last straw.

What with this and heroin, which by this time was only lasting a couple of hours before I needed my next fix, my mind was beginning to blow. I suppose you could call it a bit of a drugs cocktail and it was affecting my behaviour, which was bad enough before but now changed and became even more violent, if that was possible. If that wasn't enough, I felt now very insecure and very paranoid. Most of my violence, as I've said, was directed towards my wife. Now the violence was spreading into the execution of my crimes.

Acid, if you didn't know, is a mind drug. It affects the mind's ability to deal with reality. Hallucinations are commonplace and if you are "lucky" enough to have a "good trip" then peace and tranquility abound. On the other hand, you may be unlucky and have a "bad trip" where your worst nightmares become reality. For example, you can be walking down the street and the pavement opens up in front of you spewing out enormous flames. They reach out trying to grab you, so you turn and run, but the opening seems to chase you and there's no escape – the flames lick at you, touching you. You feel your skin beginning to burn and as you run, you turn and see yourself in a shop window. You see the skin on your face melting, dropping to the pavement revealing the bone underneath; your skull is staring at you. Believe me, although it is not actually happening your mind tells you it is. All your senses react as though they are being burned and the pain is excruciating. It is like watching a really bad horror movie. The difference is you are the star; it is real to you and there is no escape for you.

You can imagine coming out of a robbery, for example, after taking some acid and the trip turns. One minute things are OK, the next you are under attack. So what do you do? Fight back, that's what. I remember a robbery I was involved in when a small dog came running at me barking. This small animal became a roaring lion because I was tripping. So I blasted it with my gun. Needless to say there wasn't much left of it afterwards. I was becoming crazier with each passing day.

I decided I had to do something – this could not go on. It was only a matter of time before I killed someone, possibly even my wife who by now was very pregnant. I didn't want to hurt my unborn child and I knew that in time I might. I still had some humane feelings – not many, but some.

I was having nightmares regularly. Tracey would appear, begging me to join her. She looked terrible, so ugly and deformed. Was this my conscience telling me enough was enough?

I decided eventually to go for treatment. I landed up

in a hospital in southeast London where I met a fellow addict who told me of a new kind of drug treatment. He told me it was available at a private clinic and it would cost two hundred pounds a session. It was a heck of a lot of money but I believed I could raise it. He gave me the address and told me he'd heard it was very good. So here was my chance.

I found out when I got there what the treatment consisted of. The object was to get the addict to associate drugs with pain. Electrodes were attached to patients and when they wanted a fix, it would register and give the patient an electric shock. I suppose in theory it worked, but where you've got people who spend their entire waking hours searching for the biggest buzz they can find, the electric shock was a good substitute. People were spaced out all over the treatment centre. I attended twice a week for six months; my determination to change was strong and it took this long to realize the treatment wasn't working. Not only did I get a buzz from the shocks, but I realized that I wasn't changing. I still wanted drugs because when the electrodes were taken off, surprisingly enough the brain knew it wouldn't get a shock. Unless you could walk around twenty-four hours a day with it attached then it didn't do any good at all.

Besides all this I couldn't get away from crime. I had to do something to be able to pay for the treatment and crime was the only way I knew how. So after six long months of trying really hard I decided to leave. They then asked me if I would like to try Methadone as a treatment. I laughed. After six months of wasted time and money they were going to offer me this. I was already addicted to heroin and they wanted to give me another "A" listed drug which was also highly addictive. I knew that wouldn't work for me and so decided the only way to come off drugs was to do it on my own. I was disappointed, angry and not looking forward to it, but I was determined to get rid of my habit one way or another for the sake of my wife and unborn child.

I knew the pain and discomfort of going "cold turkey" would be unbearable. I'd gone through it many times before. Every time I needed a fix the withdrawals would begin – stomach cramps, cold sweats, vomiting etc. but I always had the knowledge that once I took that fix those symptoms would disappear.

The drug addict lives for the relief of those symptoms. It is not, as some think, the high they seek, it is the banishment of cold turkey. The high that is experienced only seems better because the withdrawals are more severe. Cold turkey to the drug addict is death; they don't believe they will survive it and their very existence is survival.

So I tried to go it alone. I decided that the other people who had tried and failed were doing it the wrong way. They'd always gone back to drugs whether they'd lasted six weeks or six years; they'd always gone backwards. I decided that the reason they hadn't succeeded was because they abstained totally from all drugs. I thought I would go one better.

I worked out a personal plan for my endeavour. I would stop taking heroin and if the pain became too much for me then I always had drink, speed and cannabis to pull me through. When the heroin withdrawals had gone I would wean myself away from the speed and cannabis. I would then be left with just drink which was perfectly acceptable. Looking back, it was a ridiculous way to try but I didn't want to be like everyone else. I also wanted to keep my drug crutch. At the time I don't think I would've been able to cope without anything at all.

I carried on working as much as I could and if I felt a bit down I would take some speed to pick me up again, and so on. I was surprised at how easy it was. I didn't feel half as bad as I thought I would. The one thing I didn't realize was that because I was taking other drugs the withdrawal symptoms from heroin lasted longer. I'd heard that it lasted for about three or four days. Mine lasted for a couple of months. My family thought I had gastric flu and kept asking me to go to the doctor's. I carried on feeling unwell even after I'd smoked my last little bit of cannabis. Needless to say I didn't go to the doctor's.

I thought I'd beaten it. All these other people had struggled like mad to get free but I'd licked it as easy as anything and without anybody else's help. I felt that at last I had achieved something and it was going to last. Or so I thought.

My wife has often asked me why it is that people who have survived for years without taking drugs suddenly slip back and take an overdose. The answer is simple. Our society is geared to success not failure. Many doctors don't understand the mind of an addict. They believe that once the physical dependency is over, the problem is pretty much over. The addict is not told that his/her mind is just as dependent on his body and that the dependency of the mind takes years to heal. Until it does, the addict will go on craving the drug on which it was hooked. When this happens he is told he is not normal or that he is not trying hard enough and this obviously makes the addict feel like a failure.

This happened to a girl I once knew. She'd been "clean" for ten years, helping other addicts to overcome their problems. But every time she saw somebody using a needle (jacking up) she craved it herself. She was told, and believed herself, that she wasn't trying hard enough. She battled for years to overcome this until she couldn't handle it any longer and took an overdose. She didn't think she would ever be completely free from drugs. If she had been told that her craving was completely normal and to accept that eventually it would diminish, she would still be here today. It saddens me that there is a wealth of first-hand experience in this country and yet it is not used. There are hundreds of addicts who are not using drugs any more who would be only too willing to help others. I believe we could be a great help to society and maybe give something back to it if only we were given the chance.

9

My wife finally gave birth to our first child – a boy –
a boy we named Alec. At this time I hadn't taken heroin
for over two months. After leaving the drug treatment
clinic, I'd continued taking it for over a month. Then I
decided enough was enough and I stopped. The pain
and discomfort I went through would be impossible to
put into words. When I was presented with this lovely
little baby it all seemed worthwhile. When I held him I
felt such love, it really hit me, as if someone had just
punched me in the stomach and knocked all the wind
out of me. I had closed a door inside myself so many years
before and had become so cold and uncaring that the
love I felt for this little bundle really did knock me for six.

I held him in my arms and he felt so safe, so small
and warm. I bent my head and kissed him on the fore-
head. His skin was like warm silk, so new. He opened
his eyes and our eyes met, father and son and we
instantly knew each other. He smiled up at me. People
say newborn babies can't smile, I say that's rubbish.
We were going to conquer the world together, my son
and I. His little mouth started to open and close just
like a baby bird's. I knew without being told he was
hungry. Anne held her arms out and I handed him to
her and she took him to her breast.

The nurse asked me to wait outside. I told her, "No
way, love, I want to watch him." Anne just smiled. I

even looked at her with different eyes. She was a mother. He suckled at his mother so hungrily and every now and again he would open his eyes and search out his mother's. He would stop feeding for a second, then as if satisfied she was there would start again. I was amazed; he was so small yet already he knew his mother. I reached out, offered him my finger and he grabbed it. I then spoke words that I meant for the first time in my life, "I love you, darling." He stopped eating and turned such lovely blue eyes to me and smiled – then went back to his mother's breast.

Anne said to me, "He knows who you are; he knows your voice." She later told me that after that first visit he could be fast asleep, but as soon as he heard my voice his eyes would open and he would wriggle about, waiting for me to pick him up, which I always did.

I left the hospital. I couldn't get my son or my feelings out of my mind. I went out to wet the baby's head as was customary and had a drink with my family. But it had no effect on me. No matter how much I drank I seemed to become more clear-headed than light-headed. I got fed up with this effect, said my goodnights and made my way home.

We were lucky that when we were first married, we lived with Anne's parents and then in my parents' house. They had gone to Scotland for a time, so we had the place to ourselves. My family then bought a shop with living space above, to extend the business premises. The shop was used as office space and we were given the place above it. It was an old maisonette on four floors. It was big, spacious and because money was no problem at that time we'd made it very comfortable, with a nursery all ready for the new arrival.

I arrived home and sat down in the living room. I looked out at the traffic passing below, at the people going about their daily business. I was watching and hearing everything and yet none of it penetrated my thoughts. I smiled to myself. My son wasn't even home and already he'd changed me. I sat there drinking tea. Tea!! No drugs, no drink, boy, was I changing and I was actually enjoying it.

I felt happy and contented, you see. This little baby and my wife Anne were to be my last chance. I could put my life of crime, drugs and prostitution behind me and make a fresh start. I had already been off drugs for over two months. I was still drinking, but I would slowly change that and give it up as well. I believed I could do it. I decided to start then and there. I gathered up all the booze and pills and poured them down the sink. I really felt happy with myself and life. I knew I could make it; my son had given me a chance. I'd even asked God for a peace treaty to end the war I'd declared on Him many years before.

Because of my drug addiction I was sure my child would be deformed in some way – in fact Anne had had a few problems during her pregnancy and I thought it was my fault. Two months earlier I had prayed. I didn't know how to but I asked God to make my child healthy. We didn't know at that time the effect drugs had on people. This was 1967 and we'd heard some stories about doctors prescribing drugs and babies being born deformed. So that was the basis of my prayer. I felt He had answered me as our son was perfect. I really felt at peace with the world and, for the first time, with myself.

My thoughts were interrupted by the phone ringing.

I rushed to answer it thinking it might be Anne. The sound of the voice at the other end told me it wasn't her. It was the sister of a very well-known man who had been one of my "clients" for quite some time. She wanted some company so I told her I wasn't interested any more. She promised to help me break away from the porn ring and prostitution if I went over to her place. I agreed.

So I spent the night with her and, as promised, she arranged a job for me and got a lot of people off my back. She was to remain a dear friend for many years. She had scandal and pain in her own life and later on she asked my forgiveness for helping to corrupt my young mind. I could not hate her, and years later when she asked me if I had forgiven her, I really meant it when I said yes.

The next day I went to see Anne. She was really happy because for once I was sober and at last I had a regular job and I was determined to keep it. It involved driving a large lorry and trailer down to the fruit dock at Sheerness and delivering the fruit to markets around the country. It meant a lot of driving and heavy lifting and sometimes I only got four or five hours off a day. The money was a pittance compared with what I was earning before, but for the first time in my life I felt really good about myself. The money was earned in an honest way and I was really enjoying myself. Anne was happy as well. She said I was more easygoing.

Then as suddenly as my new-found happiness had started, it ended. Our son was gone – dead. As quickly as he'd arrived he left. He was such a big healthy boy. He'd had problems teething like all babies and we had taken him to the hospital a few times with convulsions only to be told that there was nothing to worry about, he was perfectly normal. Then, one night when he was six months old I went in to check on him. He seemed so still. It wasn't until I leant over the cot that I realized he was lifeless. I called out to Anne who went to call an ambulance. I lifted him out of the cot and downstairs to the living room where I laid him on the carpet. Inside, I couldn't take in what was happening. Somehow I knew there was no hope for him but I wasn't going to give up on my son. I began to give him mouth to mouth resuscitation. I was pleading with him to wake up although there was part of me that realized he wouldn't.

We got him to the hospital and the doctors took him into a cubicle. We could hear the machinery going to work on him and it seemed like ages before the doctor came out – it was in fact only about ten or fifteen minutes – to tell us that our son was dead. Anne just sat down as though someone had knocked all the wind out of her. She reached up and took my hand. They told us we could go in and say goodbye to him, so we walked into where our son was lying. Anne picked him up and gave him a cuddle.

"This isn't our Alex; he's gone," she said. She passed him over to me and I laid him back down on the bed and wrapped him in the sheet. I couldn't believe he was dead. I picked him up again and walked towards the door. I wanted to take him home to lay him in his own little bed. This place was so cold and unfamiliar; he looked so out of place here and he felt so cold. I hugged him, opened my shirt and put him next to my skin, pulling my clothes about him to warm him up. He was so cold that I began shivering.

I heard voices telling me that I had to leave him there.

How could they? He was my child. I couldn't leave him. Anne took him from me and as she did so the doctors offered me something to drink; they said it would help. It tasted bitter and it didn't help. I looked round and he was gone – they had stolen our child.

I screamed his name only to be answered by Anne. "Angus, Angus, he's gone." Oh, no. This hurt so much, every part of my body was in pain. I had felt pain before but nothing like this. Anne held me. I suddenly realized I was crying – tears, huge wet tears and they hurt, each one hurt so much. It was as though my saviour was gone. I couldn't handle this.

We left the hospital, there was no point in staying there. We called a taxi and on the way I told Anne I would tell my parents myself and that I would drop her off at her parents' first. She asked me if I was all right. I said I was. Inside I still couldn't believe he was gone.

I thought: so, God, our truce is over is it? I felt so angry that for once I didn't know what to do. I was actually calm now – no tears or screaming, at least not on the outside. Why, God? Why my son? Why not me? I kept asking myself. He'd done nothing wrong and yet look at me, rotten to the core. He hadn't hurt anyone. I'd hurt many. The guilt and pain were unbearable.

Anne and I looked at each other then and all of a sudden it hit us. She was no longer a mother nor I a father. We both felt robbed, cheated, as if someone had come into our lives and stolen everything we'd ever cared about. That was it.

My parents took Alec's death very hard. My mother told me that it brought back the memory of the children she herself had lost. She was heartbroken. My father had worshipped Alec; he couldn't believe it. I didn't want to stay there too long. I was still finding it almost too hard to bear myself and to be surrounded by relatives who were all tearful was something I didn't want to face. So I said goodbye to my family. I would go to God's house and speak with Him. We might be able to come to a deal.

The door of the local church was open so I went in. I went to the front and stood there. I felt so alone it was as though I was the last person left in the world. There wasn't a sound in that place. I felt in so much pain – and tired, so very tired. I sat down on the steps leading up to the altar and rested my head in my hands. I don't know how long I sat there, but I cried; the tears just seemed to go on and on.

"Oh, God", I said, "Please forgive me for going to war with You. Please give me back my son. There is nothing I won't do for You. Anything. Just let me have him back."

I waited. I was lost. Without Alec I could not make it; he was my last chance to be normal. There was no answer, just silence. I screamed out, "You bastard, I'm going to get You. Someone will pay. I swear someone will pay."

My temper normally made me feel better, but this time, nothing. I walked out of the church a totally broken man. It was getting light by now. Another day was beginning although I felt as if time had stood still.

I convinced myself it was all a mistake, that I would get home and everything would be normal. Anne and Alec would be there waiting for me. I was wrong.

The funeral was behind us and not long afterwards my father died. I felt then and do now that he never got over my son's death. He had been ill anyway but I think it was just too much for him; he just gave up.

I didn't go back to crime or drugs. I had said sorry to God for my outburst and I still felt that somehow He would give me back our child. Anne was coping well. I think because I was grieving she felt she had to be strong, and she was.

We moved out of our house; we couldn't stay there, it was too painful. We were given a small one-bedroomed flat by the council in Paradise Street, Bermondsey, overlooking the river. It was at the top of a five-floor old block of flats and it cost all of seven shillings and sixpence – that's approximately thirty-seven and a half pence in new money. It was only small but we liked it. There we were on our own and Anne announced she was pregnant again.

It was only about ten months since Alec had died. The doctors had told us to try for another child as soon as possible, which is what we did. I was very happy but at the same time worried that the same would happen to this child as the last. I tried to convince Anne that nothing would happen and she tried to convince me that everything was OK. I must say she was one strong lady. She sailed through the pregnancy and presented me with a lovely baby girl. This one we called Tanya and she was really lovely. I was sure in some way my prayers had been answered and I had been given back my son. I did not know how, I just knew I had. I was really pleased – she was a lovely little girl and we were very happy.

I had stayed off drugs and had not gone back to crime and it had paid off. I still had a chance to make a good life, a normal life. Yet I could not shake off this feeling that all was not well – a sense of foreboding that something was going to happen.

I had just lost my job so I had to go down to the National Assistance Board (now called the DHSS) for some money. I had told Anne I had lost my job for refusing to do extra work but I had in fact been given the sack for fighting. I had been offered some drugs at work and because I wanted to stay "clean" I refused.

This guy wouldn't go away, and on this particular day he came on a bit strong with me so we landed up fighting. Needless to say I was given the sack with no money.

Anne told me to take a couple of weeks off from looking for work as I looked tired. She was right; I had been working long hours, plus I wanted to spend some time with her and the baby. I decided the next day I would go to the NAB and put in a claim. We had also decided to go to the south coast for a few days, to her mother's caravan. Anne felt the break would do us good.

We went to bed that night and I lay there thinking. Things were not so bad. We had a little car, a nice flat, a little money and a smashing baby daughter. Perhaps my nagging worry had no foundation after all.

When I awoke the next morning, Anne and Tanya were still asleep. I left them, got dressed, had a cup of tea and made my way to our local NAB.

I arrived there about ten a.m. and ran into my brother George. He asked me if I wanted a pint of beer before going in. George knew the manager of the pub next door so we were let in before they opened. He served us with a pint of beer each. It was nice and quiet sitting there. George asked if everything was OK. I told him things were going well and that we were going to the coast for a few days.

He said, "Don't get Anne pregnant again; you know how that sea air affects you." It was a standing joke between us. Each time we went to the coast Anne came back pregnant. We finished our beers and made our way next door to put our claims in.

I made my claim and sat down, expecting a long wait. If you've ever been to these offices you'll know they are not well known for speed. Five hours is classed as fast, believe me. So you can imagine how surprised I was when George told me they were calling my name and I'd only been waiting fifteen minutes.

I went up to the counter and they handed my money to me. They told me I had to go home because there was a problem. I turned around to see George speaking to two policemen. They started to walk towards me. I took a step back and raised my fists. I thought they were after me for something. George assured me that wasn't why they were there, that it was Anne. I asked one of the policemen what was wrong but he just kept looking away. George told me they would take me home, to go with them and everything would be OK. So that's just what I did.

I walked through the front door and was met by my father-in-law. He didn't have to say a word. I knew. "It's Tanya, isn't it?" He just nodded, tears streaming down his face. It's not nice to see a man in such pain. I didn't cry, shout or even make a sound, just turned around and walked back through my door closing it behind me.

I had tried to come out of my old lifestyle and failed.

I wanted nothing more to do with the normal world. Give me drugs, prostitution and crime any day. No more mister nice guy. Enough was enough.

It seemed that when I had really tried to change I was hurt more than at any other period in my life. I'd had not one but three children die on me. Some people can't handle one. I had three to contend with.

I was going back where I belonged, in the gutter.

10

I thought that going back behind my closed doors would be easy. It wasn't. I was used to blocking things out, but try as I might I couldn't block out Tanya and Alec. They were part of me as much as I was a part of them. Even my faithful drugs, booze and sex didn't work. The harder I tried the more my memories of them came back; they filled my life.

Six months after Tanya died I decided I'd had enough. I was going to end it all and meet this guy called God, who as far as I was concerned was my tormentor. I would have it out with Him once and for all.

I made sure there was enough money in the electric meter and switched on the light. It was all set. I got myself a chair and climbed on it, then took out the light bulb. I'd half-filled a bowl of water, just to make sure I had enough and stuck my hand in it making sure it was dripping wet. I then lifted my hand to the light socket and stuck my finger into it. Nothing happened. I wiggled my finger around hoping to get a better connection; still nothing. There I was, balancing on the chair with my finger stuffed in the light socket, a wet finger at that, waiting for the flash to end all flashes and there wasn't even a sizzle. Blasted electric company, I thought. Never there when you want them.

I wondered if I'd already gone, if it had already happened. Was I dead? I remembered that people who had been electrocuted had their hair burned, so I felt mine. No, that was OK. I was coming to the conclusion that I was still alive when Anne walked through the door.

"What the hell are you doing?" she screamed. I hadn't heard her come in and she scared the living daylights out of me. I overbalanced and fell off the chair.

"Bloody fool, you scared the hell out of me," I shouted at her. She asked again what I was doing. I said nothing. She got up on the chair and put the light-bulb back in and . . . on came the light.

"God isn't ready for you yet, love," she said. "Stay with me for now, eh love?"

I just nodded. I was disappointed in one way that my suicide attempt had failed but in another way I was somewhat taken aback. I wasn't dead and I should've been. I now know that God had directly intervened and saved my life. There was nothing at all wrong with the light and yet when I'd tried to kill myself it didn't work. That was the second time. The first time was when I was in a coma and He spoke to me directly. I was a little lost. I really didn't know what to think. My mind was in turmoil.

We were due to move that week to a new house. After Tanya's death the council had decided to move us to another place, so my mind was taken up with packing. I pushed the whole incident to the back of my mind and we moved to our new house.

It was a new maisonette with its own bathroom. Anne was delighted. I was pleased but I was also sorry to leave our little flat. I felt I was leaving part of me behind.

Not long after we moved, I had a complete break-down. Anne had to call in the doctor. She told me later that she had found me fully clothed in the bath having a wash. She said I was talking but she couldn't understand anything I was saying. I was completely incoherent. The only thing she did understand was that I told her I wanted to save energy by bathing and washing my clothes at the same time. I suppose I had completely flipped.

Anne and the doctor decided it would be best if I was moved to a psychiatric hospital not only for my safety but also for others'. It was then the boys in blue arrived. I don't know what happened next but I saw one of the policemen flying across the room. I was told afterwards that I really went crazy. I was injected with something, what it was I didn't know, but everything seemed to slow down. People spoke to me but their faces seemed huge and their voices slow and slurred. I started to laugh, things seemed so funny; everything was going through my mind at once – faces and voices from the past, some of them long dead and others I wished were. They took me downstairs to a private car. The police seemed to enrage me for some reason so they were kept out of the way to keep me calm.

I was on my way to the loony bin. They always said the little men in white coats would come for me. I kept wondering where they were. I asked but got no reply. Oh well, it didn't matter really. I was on my way.

We arrived at the hospital through old Victorian gates. There were gargoyles on top of the pillars staring down at me. My friends have come to welcome me, I thought. The staff nurse who greeted me wasn't much better. I wouldn't like to get on the wrong side of her

– if I could find it. My thoughts at that time weren't rational to say the least. I was like a person who had just been given laughing gas; everything was amusing. She showed me to a ward and demanded my clothes. I said, "No, they won't fit you," and promptly climbed into bed. This nurse and I were to become deadly enemies and she never did get my clothes.

I don't remember my wife or the doctor leaving as I fell into a deep sleep. How long I slept I don't know, but a nurse of about thirty woke me to give me a couple of pills and some clear, bitter-tasting liquid. I later found out it was triptosol (liquid handcuffs), a drug widely used in places such as these and in prisons. It is a drug that is used to keep you calm so you won't cause any trouble; in other words it puts your brain out of gear. Not a very nice drug at all, with long-term side effects.

This nurse was called Jean and we were to become very good friends as time went on. She informed me that the doctor wanted to see me. I asked why and she said he needed to find out what my problems were. I told her I wanted a bath first and she agreed. She fetched me a dressing gown and a pair of pyjamas and showed me to the bathroom. She told me to leave my clothes on the chair. Why was everyone after my clothes? I asked myself.

I worked out that they could be after my body. That I wasn't too bothered about; after all everyone had had a bit of it anyway, a few more wouldn't hurt. But I couldn't understand why they wanted my clothes. I decided in the end that whether they wanted them or not they were not having them. They were mine and nobody was going to get their hands on them. I looked around. Where could I put them? I noticed the window.

All the other windows had bars on them, but this one didn't. Had they overlooked it? My mind boggled. I tried the window and it slid open. I waited for flashing lights or bells or something, but there was nothing. I climbed out and into the garden that surrounded the hospital. Now I had to hunt around for somewhere to put my clothes – I'd make sure no one got their hands on them. I walked over to some trees, dug a hole and buried them then climbed back into the bathroom.

When it was noticed that my clothes were missing, all hell broke loose. I didn't know what all the fuss was about. Jean my friendly nurse told me they were concerned that if they couldn't find them and another patient was to get hold of them he could get out. I asked, "Have they got a key as well? Even if they did get my clothes, how would they get past all the locked doors?" I was to find out that there were ways out and I was to slip in and out at will.

My first meeting with the doctor in charge of the unit was not a success. I thought he was in a worse state than the patients. I walked into his office. He was sitting at his desk wearing a T-shirt and a pair of shorts. He had a mop of hair and seemed to speak to a large teddy bear sitting in a chair next to him.

He asked, "And how are we today?"

Before I had a chance, Teddy answered for me. "OK thank you."

Oh no, I thought, I'm hearing a stuffed bear talking to me now. It took me a while to realize that it was the doctor talking and not my mind playing tricks on me as I was having trouble with hallucinations anyway.

I really told this man where to get off.

"Calm down, calm down, Angus," he said. "I will

increase your drugs to keep you calmer. I'm only trying to put you at ease; that's why I dress as I do and have Teddy here as a therapeutic aid."

Oh, well, I thought, how silly, why hadn't I thought of that? People do go about in December dressed in shorts and T-shirt speaking to a teddy.

He opened his desk drawer, took out a bottle of Scotch and took a swig. I asked him if it was what I thought it was. He asked me if I wanted some and handed me the bottle. We spent the next hour drinking and he told me all his problems. Yep, I felt this guy could really help me – like a hole in the head.

My problems became worse. I was hallucinating more and more. One incident sticks in my mind especially. I was watching television in the lounge and all of a sudden my picture appeared on the screen. They said I was being hunted for the murder of my children. This frightened the life out of me to say the least. Nobody else in the room seemed to have noticed, so I crawled out on my hands and knees. Jean met me and asked what I was doing. I told her what had happened. She said she would help to sneak me back to my room where I would be safe and no one would find me.

It was decided that another visit to the doctor was needed. Great, I thought, I could be doing with another drink – save me sneaking down to the pub. I was always sneaking out of the bathroom window, getting my clothes and going to the pub or to get some drugs. Jean knew about this but never gave me away.

So, off I trotted to the doctor and Teddy. Teddy asked me why I felt that people in power were persecuting me. I told Teddy over a drink some of the things I had been involved in with those "fine upstanding people", some of whom were helping to run the country. Teddy and the doctor really flew at me. I was informed by Teddy that I was going to be taken off all medication for a time to help bring me back to reality. I thought, Teddy, your days are numbered. I was going to kill Teddy. Bastard, I thought, I'll give him Teddy.

That night I sneaked into my doctor's office and there was Teddy lying out on the couch smiling up at me with his little pyjamas on, head on a pillow and a pretty quilt covering him.

"Hello, Teddy," I said. "Bloody hell, I'm as bad as him."

I pulled back the quilt, took Teddy over to the desk and chopped off his head, arms and legs. Each one I placed strategically around the room, with the head placed on the blotting pad in the middle of the desk facing the door. Each joint I smeared with tomato sauce to make it look realistic. I must admit, it did look good. I crept out, saying goodbye to Teddy as I went. Funny he didn't answer me. I got back into bed and waited for morning.

Jean woke me up. "Morning, Angus," and gave me a quick kiss. I looked at her and burst out laughing.

"What's so funny?" she said with a puzzled expression.

"Just wait and see," I said. We didn't have long to wait.

There was a loud scream and we both rushed into the corridor. There was my doctor with his shorts and T-shirt on, knees knocking, crying tears of rage. He pointed at me.

"I'll get you for this," he shouted.

"What's up, Doc?" I said. The look on his face finished me off. I just fell about laughing.

Jean still didn't know what it was all about. The doctor told her to look in his office at what this vicious man had done. She did as he asked, saw Teddy then turned her back on the doctor.

"Oh, Angus, why did you kill Teddy?" she said, and walked away shoulders shaking with laughter. But the doctor was too angry to notice. He said he would get me and he did. That day I was given my first electric shock treatment.

I know the reason he gave me the treatment was revenge for Teddy because I wasn't even told beforehand what they were going to do. I thought I was going for some sort of scan. The first I knew about it was when the electricity surged through my body. They didn't seek my permission at any time. When it was over they unstrapped me and there was my doctor smiling at me. They thought I was weaker than I was.

"Well, Angus, feel better now?" He was standing there with a new teddy in his arms.

What started as a joke had now become war. I don't know if it was the man or the teddy he was holding that made me explode, but I lunged at him and got my hands round his throat and squeezed. The orderlies beat me off and injected me with something. How long I had my hands round his throat I don't know, but I came to myself in a padded cell racked with pain. My jaw, two of my fingers and a toe were broken, and I was covered in bruises. The door opened and there stood Jean. I tried to stand up to greet her but fell over.

She cried, "Oh, Angus, what have they done to you?" I hugged her and she told me I'd been unconscious for two days and helped me back to my room.

Enough was enough. I told her I was signing myself

out and going home. She said OK and helped me to dress. So I took my leave of the hospital.

Jean took me to her house and cleaned me up. I spent a couple of days with her to recuperate, then she took me home. She explained to Anne what had happened then left.

As quickly as I had had my breakdown I seemed to pull myself out of it. I was back as if I had been asleep and awakened refreshed. But deep down I knew I wasn't right. The war with God would go on but I felt that I just wanted to be left alone. I was slowly going off people.

I went back to crime and I was becoming more violent. I was beginning to hurt people in the robberies and burglaries I was committing and starting to enjoy it. I could see no way out. I was arrested for little things – nothing serious – and I was paying off various police officers to turn a blind eye on my activities. Soon I decided I'd had enough of that and refused to pay them any more.

Then one day two CID officers, whom I hadn't stopped paying, visited me to tell me that the word had gone out to arrest me any way they could. They informed me that unless I quietened down my criminal activities they would arrest me and if it meant fitting me up they would. I was rocking the boat too much. I took back the money I had given them and laughed. I told them I didn't give a damn and threw them out, not very gently I might add.

Anne was terrified. She couldn't believe what she had just seen and heard. She begged me to go back to hospital to get help. She was coming to the end of the line;

she didn't know what to do any more. Our marriage was now in name only and we both knew it. We were both glad when it finally came to an end.

It was to be a further year before I was arrested, but that was a very eventful year. I met a girl called Karen at a party. She was an American student, nineteen years old and living in London. We became lovers and very close. She invited me to a party but I was the only one invited. She greeted me at the door naked with a party hat on and the words "You're going to be a dad" blazoned across her stomach.

I was stunned but at the same time really happy. It was now nearly five years since the death of Tanya and seven years since the death of Alec and I thought, well, they say third time lucky. Perhaps for me it would be fourth time lucky. We decided she would have the baby in England. She'd asked me to go back with her to America, but I wanted to wait around for a while to give me time to make some money so that I could leave Anne financially secure.

I was excited at the prospect of a new country and a new wife. Things would be all right this time. I worked even harder now. I wanted this new adventure to happen sooner rather than later. I was sleeping with more women and making more pornographic films. I was making as much money as I could, but I was also taking more drugs.

The time came for Karen to have her baby, so she went to stay with her aunt who lived in the country. She gave birth to a lovely little girl called Jane who had huge brown eyes and brown hair.

When Karen came back to London, Jean very kindly

put her and the baby up for a while. They got on really well — two mistresses together, one young the other older — yet they were like sisters and Jean loved the baby. I spent two weeks there with them all day and all night. But Anne was beginning to get suspicious that something was going on. So to keep the peace I stayed away for a couple of months, only seeing them now and again.

I went over one day. I hadn't seen Karen or the baby for nearly two weeks and I was dying to see them. I burst into the room. Karen was standing there and I rushed over and hugged her.

"We can leave soon, darling. OK, love?" She just stared at me and I knew something was wrong. I held her at arm's length. "Karen, what's the matter, love?"

Jean walked in dressed in black. For the first time I noticed Karen's clothing was dark too. My stomach started to knot.

"Who's died, anyone I know?" I joked, although at that moment I didn't want to joke at all. Realization came slowly. Karen hung her head. She would not look at me.

Jean was the one to break the awful silence. "Karen, have you told him?"

"Told me what? Will someone tell me what's going on?" I had a sense of foreboding by this time.

"Jane is dead. We've just been to the funeral."

I couldn't believe what had happened. This was the fourth baby to die. When was this going to end? It was my fault. Every child I'd fathered had died. There wasn't much known about cot death at that time so I suppose my thoughts were normal. Now, however, more is known and I don't feel so bad.

Karen then dropped the other bombshell. She was pregnant again. She said it was due to our wild two weeks together after Jane was born. She told me she had spoken to her aunt and Jean about it and had decided to fly home to America to have the baby. She had also decided not to come back afterwards.

She left almost immediately. I took her to the airport. I wondered what would happen to our dream of living in her country. She didn't mention it and I didn't ask. We said our goodbyes and she left, gone from my life, along with my hope for a normal life.

The very next day I was arrested, not that I cared very much. Anne couldn't understand why I went along so meekly, as though I had resigned myself to it. In a way I had. How could I tell her about baby Jane, let alone Karen or how I felt? I was dead inside and finished. It was over for me.

11

1974, the year that was to change my life yet again.

I was in a pub having a drink, trying to put things together in my mind. Karen had gone back to America, our child was dead, so were my other three children. It seemed that anything I touched died or went wrong; twenty-four years of age and I was a walking disaster area. Then a guy walked in, a friend of Gino's. "Hello, Gus." I didn't even look up from my drink. He carried on speaking. I wasn't really listening, I only caught a word here and there. Then I heard the word "arrested".

"Hang on," I said. "Who's been arrested?"

"You, Gus," he replied.

I laughed. "What for?"

He told me about a young girl who had been raped the week before. He said I was going to do time for it. He said it was down to me.

I knew the case he was talking about. A week before the police had pulled me in for questioning about some other crimes in the area and they wanted me to give them information. I told them no. They tried for four hours to get me to talk and when I didn't they released me. As a parting shot they told me that if I didn't change my mind they would arrest me for the assault on this little girl. I wanted to laugh, but the humour that had kept me going for all those years had suddenly deserted me. I told them to do their worst. In a funny way I was relieved. I could feel that the end was near.

I thought of all the times I had witnessed rapes in the past and how many times I had been raped I couldn't count. Now they were fitting me up for this. Bastards, I thought. I jumped up and head-butted the guy and had the pleasure of feeling his nose break. As he went down so did my fist and I broke his jaw. Then went his ribs.

I bent down and whispered, "Now you have something to nick me for, you bastard." I spat at him, then walked calmly out of the pub. Nobody interfered. This was the rough East End of London; one against one and everybody looked away. I went home and the police came for me an hour later.

I was held for possibly three days. I say possibly because I was withdrawing from drugs at the time, so I can't remember the exact time I was there. I remember I was beaten quite severely while being questioned. I was shown heroin and told that if I confessed they would give it to me. There came a time when I couldn't take any more, so I signed their statement and was remanded in custody on a charge of unlawful sex with a minor. I really found that amusing after what I had been involved in. I thought they really wouldn't have the nerve to charge me with this. My solicitor will get statements as to where I was, I thought, and they will have to release me. That wasn't to be. After many months on remand in Brixton prison, I found I quite liked it. I liked being alone. I was the same as everyone else.

After the police had finished with me I was in a terrible state and because of this, my history of drink and drug problems and my stay in the mental hospital, I was put into F wing, the medical wing. Mad as they were in there, I fitted in nicely. Says a lot for me at the time, doesn't it? Nobody bothered me in there. I was left to get on and do my own thing. Apart from a half-hour walk twice a day, weather permitting, and going down to the hotplate for my meals which I ate in my cell, I could close my door and I was alone. I was still given all the drugs I needed – they even delivered to my door three times a day. I could lie on my bunk, put on my radio, take my gear and for the first time in seventeen years nobody bothered me for sex. I was left completely alone with no pressure from my wife or family. This was for me. I loved being in prison, crazy as that may sound. For me it was like paradise, apart from the crazies. I thought even they were better than the so-called normal people I had known on the outside.

My trial approached and I wasn't bothered one way or another. My attitude was to let them get on with their games as long as I was left alone. Just before my trial was due to start I was paid a visit by a Home Office man I had known on and off for a couple of years. He informed me it had been agreed that if I pleaded guilty I would be sentenced to eight years. If I fought the case, however, other charges would be brought in and he mentioned quite a few. I would get fifteen to twenty years at least, maybe more. He also told me that my involvement in porn and prostitution would come out in court and wondered out loud if my old mum would survive it. He thought not. He thought about my *mother*. I wondered if *I* would survive it. He told me to think very seriously about it and to look on the bright side. Eight years wasn't a long time and with parole I could be out in two years. He pushed across a large chunk of dope. I asked him if it was for me. He told me it was an advance.

The prison officer came and took me back to my cell. He'd seen the cannabis passed to me, so I waited for them to come and search my cell. They didn't come, so I sat back on my bunk and rolled myself a joint. I fell asleep thinking about what I would do only to dream of all the ghosts in my life.

I had been told that I would be going to court in two weeks' time. I was surprised to see my solicitor the very next day. He told me that my case had been brought forward to the following day. He informed me that the barrister who was going to defend me had suddenly withdrawn from my case, that another barrister had taken over and that he would see me in court the next day.

My big day came. I was waiting in the cells below the Old Bailey. It was an imposing place, big old and cold, not very impressive really. I had been taking dope all night and still was so I had trouble focusing on what was happening. The officer came for me and told me my barrister was there to see me. I thought of Perry Mason or Rumpole of the Bailey. Who did I get? A fat little man with fishy eyes who seemed more out of his head than I was.

"I've read all the papers, Angus," he said. "You've got no chance; just plead guilty as you've been told. Throw yourself on the mercy of the court. Good man, see you upstairs." Then he was gone. That was to be my Perry Mason, heaven help me. With that I was led up the stairs to the court. I suddenly realized that I didn't have a clue as to what was going on. I was totally confused, it was all moving too fast for me. All I could think about was that saying, stop the world I want to get off.

Next thing I knew there was a man in a wig and long coat speaking to me. "How do you plead, guilty or not guilty?"

I replied, "How about insanity?" I was the only one who laughed. There was just silence. I felt terrible. I just wanted to creep away so no one would notice me, but I had nowhere to go. The judge was looking at me again, everyone was. Where was my wife and family? There were no friendly faces – only cold unfriendly eyes.

"Mr Urquhart will you answer, guilty or not?" It was the judge again.

I said, "No."

"No what?" The judge was beginning to get a bit shirty by now.

"I will not plead anything," I replied. "I'm not represented here."

The judge pointed to the fat little man with the fishy eyes. He was looking even smaller now. I think he was trying to slide under his table hoping no one would notice him.

I pointed at him. "He's nothing like Perry Mason and he's not defending me."

The judge adjourned the case. I thought I had won. I was taken back to Brixton prison only to be informed that I would be going back the next day for another performance.

You may think I was being offhanded or not taking it all seriously enough. To be honest I think I was past that. I had no real idea of what was happening around me. I had reverted to being a little boy where the grown-ups were trying to get me to do something I didn't want to. I knew eventually I would have to do as they said and they would leave me alone. I was just being awkward for a little while. It was a no-win situation as far as I was concerned. I was just protesting a bit to let them know that I wasn't pleased. I was convinced that it would soon be over and they would let me go home. This time I was wrong. They didn't intend to let me go anywhere except prison.

Anne and my family were not in court because they hadn't been told I was there. The first Anne heard about it was when she visited me in prison, only to be told that I'd gone to court. She rushed over to the court and was told I had just left and that I would be coming back the following day.

After speaking with an officer about what I should do, I decided to make a deal and go for the easy option. Some easy option! The next day I went back to court and pleaded guilty, at least that's what I was told. I don't actually remember anything about it. So there I was, serving an eight-year sentence for a crime I didn't commit. What I didn't know then was that this decision I made all those years ago was to come back and haunt me many times for the next eighteen years.

I will not go into detail about the case and the evidence as the space I have got in this book wouldn't be enough and wouldn't do "justice" to it. This I hope will come in a later book. This conviction not only affected me but also my second wife and son in ways I will go into later on. Now, though, when we see people getting their names cleared we both smile at each other, thinking how great it would be if that were me and I was getting my name cleared.

So I started my life as a convicted prisoner. The months I'd spent on remand had prepared me for prison life and at the beginning it wasn't very different. I arrived at the reception area, stripped off my clothes and all my possessions were taken. I was given a bed roll, blankets, sheets, bed cover, a prison uniform and a white card which meant I was Church of England. This card had my prison number on it, my name and sentence. Then I was taken over to A wing – the reception wing – to be documented, told prison rules, allocated a prison in which the sentence would be served and see the welfare officer. An officer gave me a booklet about parole and my normal release date without parole. I was given a blank piece of letter paper to write to my wife, a visiting order and a pep talk. It was like a conveyor belt, one in one out. The last person to see was the prison chaplain, then at last you'd be shown to your cell.

I didn't go through most of this process because of my slightly eccentric behaviour. A prisoner called me a sex case. I didn't know what it meant, but I didn't like the sound of it, so I head-butted him. I'd learned while in Brixton that prison is like the streets. If threatened hit first worry later. The prison officers grabbed me and threw me into a little box with a seat in it. I heard one of them say, "He's the nutter, he should be going over to the hospital, not normal location." The guy I'd attacked was very nervous, "Wish someone had told me," he said.

An officer opened the door and there stood a very shaky con with a plate and a cup of tea. I growled at them showing my teeth. The door closed very quickly then opened again. I growled again but this time there was an officer standing there in a white coat, a hospital screw.

"What do I call you then? Rover or what?" he asked.

I smiled, "Rover will be fine."

He snapped his fingers, "Come on Rover. Walkies."

I like this guy, I thought. He seemed OK. He took me over to the hospital and put me into a cell. It was quite cosy – different – from the cells in Brixton. He gave me some tea and some medicine.

"OK lad," he said, "Settle down, get into bed and have a nice kip. I'll be back for you in the morning." He went to leave, then stopped. He asked me if I smoked. I said yes and he threw me some tobacco and a few matches.

I smiled, "Thanks a lot."

We became good friends. I'll call him Mr C. He was OK.

I got into bed, rolled a cigarette and lay in the dark drinking my tea. It had been a busy day. How I could relax. It was over, or was it? I slept thinking of my children and how they would have been. Happy, I know that, strong and happy. No problems. I would have protected them. Yes, I would have looked after them.

I spent the next month in the hospital. It was quiet and the other cons were OK. A nice old guy, well he was old to me, started to teach me chess. He would bring me cups of tea and coffee – he seemed all right.

After about a week Mr C. came in. "Your mate brought your tea, has he, Gus?"

"Yes, guv," I said, taking a sip of my tea.

"Do you know who he is?" he asked. I shook my head. "That's Graham Young, the mass poisoner." I spat out the tea I had just drunk. I thought he was joking but he assured me he wasn't.

Just then Young walked in, chessboard in one hand, box of pieces in the other and I asked him if he really was Graham Young.

He smiled and said, "That's me." He was such a little thin guy, I was amazed. He said, "Don't worry, Gus. I only poison family and friends."

I told him, "If you poison me I'll break your neck."

He smiled. "If I poison you, Gus, you'll be dead." There was no answer to that, was there?

Over the next eight months we became good friends and he didn't try to poison me. I suppose he couldn't have felt as close to me as I did to him. He was a very sad guy and over the months told me a lot about himself, but that's another story. He's dead now and I hope he's found the peace he wanted.

In the first four or five months of my sentence, what they had done to me didn't really hit me. I was still dealing dope. I was on my own with nobody to bother me, or so I thought. You see, they had arrested me just after Jane died and I had gone into a world deep inside myself where for a time I was safe. As far as I was concerned, my children were not dead. They were alive and well. I had switched off my mind. I couldn't take any more. Four of my children had died and Karen had gone back to America carrying another child. Yes, the charge I was on was a serious one, a terrible crime, I knew that. I had been on the receiving end enough times and I was beginning to think that I had been raped again, this time by the legal system. But what to do about it was something else.

I started to make enquiries and some of the evidence I uncovered about the offence I had apparently committed really surprised me. Statements went missing and other things just didn't add up. Oh, boy, I thought. Was I going to make trouble! Or so I thought. I was streetwise, but in the corridors of power I was like a lamb being led to the slaughter. I was green. These people had had hundreds of years' experience of covering things up and twisting things round to suit their own ends. This was going to be a hard fight. Everything I did they seemed to know about and were always one step ahead.

It was around this time that Mr C. went on leave. I told him I had decided not to take a holiday. I was going to stay home and be lazy. While he was away one of my least favourite officers took over. He looked a bit like the P.O. in *Porridge*, with little beady eyes. We didn't like each other at all. He loved the sound of his own voice and giving orders, and I loved to wind him up.

One day we got into a rather heated argument and it finished up with me emptying a full chamber pot over his head. My feet made their way to the punishment block in A wing without touching the ground and I was helped into the cell with a boot here and a punch there. They were not amused. I lost twenty-eight days' remission (time taken off a sentence for good behaviour; a third of a sentence is automatically taken off and if you misbehave, then a proportion is added on again. Complicated, isn't it?) So I'd now lost seven months altogether. The governor informed me that I would be in real trouble if I carried on this way and that I'd been placed on report forty-two times. He asked me what I had to say.

I told him, "If I'm not careful, you know, I'll land up in prison, won't I guv?" He didn't find it funny and took another seven days away for offensive behaviour. I told him to go for double or quits and again my feet didn't touch the ground on the way back to my cell. The door slammed. Bastard, I thought. I wanted to cry but stopped myself. I sat in the corner on the floor feeling really down. Me and my big mouth. I could've kicked myself. You see, despite the couldn't-care-less attitude I presented to the world, inside I was breaking up. I no longer enjoyed prison. I wanted out, yet now I had nearly six years to serve instead of five. I had this self-destruct button inside me and I kept pushing it. Was there no end to this nightmare I was in? It had gone on since I was seven. When would it end?

A few days later, without warning, my cell door burst open and I was hit with something very hard. I curled up in a ball to try and protect myself. These were not other inmates, they were prison officers and there were four or five of them. I heard the unmistakable rattle of their key chains and saw their gleaming boots. I thought I was going to die. So this is how it ends. I felt as if I was going down a dark tunnel and it was getting darker and longer and there was no light at the end – just darkness and a strange quietness. There were sounds but I couldn't quite make them out. Then I realized they were the sound of blows raining down on me. I no longer felt them but I could hear them. I tried to laugh but my mouth was full of blood and it came out in a gurgle.

It was then I heard voices from a long way off at first but getting louder. "Scream you bastard, scream."

I realized the voices were talking to me and managed

to croak, "Fuck off, bastards." I received another kick. Boy, I felt that one. The pain was so bad that my insides seemed to explode. I gritted my teeth. I would not scream. No way. If I am dying I'll do it my way, smiling. My intention was to show them that I wasn't beaten and that I never would be.

A voice spoke to me. "You're raking up too much dirt. Stop your appeal or you'll get more of the same. We can even get you in here, don't you forget that."

I summoned up all my strength and spat into his screaming face, shouting another obscenity. He kicked me again. This time there was no pain – only blackness falling. I remember thinking all this was for pouring my chamber pot over that screw, then there was nothing.

I woke up back in the hospital to find that my injuries had been received by falling downstairs. Mr C. who was back on duty by now asked me what had happened. I said, "Well, I fell down the stairs, ran back up and fell down again. After this had happened a few dozen times, they brought me here."

He smiled. "Sorry, Gus, I *thought* you'd been beaten. So you were then?"

"Yes, I was, Mr C.," I replied. He asked me why, so I told him he didn't want to know and he just nodded. He told me my wife was waiting to see me and then left. Nothing more was mentioned about it again. It was as though it had never happened.

The next year was spent going from hospital to the wing to the block. I lost count of the amount of times I'd been placed on report. They even moved me around, a few days in one prison in one part of the country, then back to the Scrubs. Backwards and forwards, a few kickings and beatings – I was getting nowhere. I was paid a visit and told if I behaved I would go to Maidstone prison in Kent but if I screwed up any more they would send me to Parkhurst on the Isle of Wight and there I would stay.

Anne asked me to try. She'd been all over the country visiting me and she was getting very fed up with it all. She wanted me to stay in one place so that she knew where to go. I agreed to give it a try which is what I did.

Just before I left for Maidstone I was given my first parole review. The man from the Home Office said I had to admit my guilt and show remorse, so I did just that. I told him a little bit about what I'd been involved in. He replied by saying I couldn't put things like that in my parole review. So I told him what he could with parole, I didn't want it. He smiled and said I would change my mind. He was wrong. I didn't. So I left Wormwood Scrubs and London to make my way to the wilds of Kent. This move was to help change my life for the better. I didn't know that at the time or how long it would take.

I arrived at Maidstone prison. From the outside it looked no different from all the other prisons I'd been to, but there the resemblance ended. Once inside I was amazed. I was put into Thanet Wing, the long-term wing. It was so clean. The whole prison was clean. There was no smell of stale urine and sweat that seemed to permeate every other prison I'd been to. The smell stayed on clothes, bedding and even in hair and could not be got rid of.

I met for the first time since my sentence began a

different kind of prison governor. Here was a man who was strict but fair. One of the big differences was that he treated inmates like human beings. I couldn't handle it to begin with. Officers and the governor addressed me by my Christian name and not by a number. I was forever looking for a catch. What was the gimmick and what would it cost me? Because you never get something for nothing in prison? I didn't know then that the governor, Peter Timms, who would later become a Methodist minister, would not only become my counsellor but also a very dear friend. The small seeds he sowed then in me would grow and change me forever.

Peter and I became involved in a war, not one that either of us recognized, but was there nevertheless. The one thing that didn't change, however, was the unseen, unspoken violence that was always there in me under the surface. I still carried a blade, still blocked up my cell door so that no surprise visitors could crash in. My drug involvement became deeper. Even sixteen years ago a lot of money was to be made in prison from drugs and I was earning. With it came fights and stabbings. The governor and officers waged a constant battle to stop drugs getting in. They found and plugged one hole and we found another.

I was also having trouble with prison "queens". These were men who, when outside had a wife and children, but once in prison would bully or bribe young prisoners to make themselves available for sex. These were the people I found the hardest to understand or forgive. On the one hand they would insult and hurt prisoners who were in for sexual crimes, grassing or mugging. They were the aristocrats of crime, if you like, the bank robbers, burglars, blackmailers, extortionists.

Once in prison they gang up, sometimes in groups of five or six, against the defenceless ones and brutally rape them. These same people call sexual offenders "nonces" or "perverts". Can anybody tell me what makes them different? Rape is rape whatever the circumstances and it's a terrible crime. The one on the receiving end never quite gets over it. He's got to learn to live with it. I was in prison for a sexual crime – OK – but a crime I hadn't committed. I had, however, committed so many more crimes, introduced other children and adults into porn and prostitution. Even though I was guilty of these crimes it didn't help me to come to terms with the fact that I'd been fitted up. What made it worse was that the people who locked me up for breaking the law had themselves twisted and broken the law to put me away. As far as I was concerned that was double standards. The more I thought about it the more bitter I became. I was trying hard to make sense of my life, where I was going wrong and how I could change.

Peter was telling me that I could change and yet I had lots of pressures on me to remain the same – inmates chasing me for drugs, queens after me for my body and men in power telling me to toe the line and keep quiet or else.

I decided, however, to try and took up prison education. I surprised myself by doing rather well and began to think that maybe there *was* another way.

I also met up with a guy called Joe who started to tell me about the love of Jesus and how He loved and cared for me. I wanted to believe him, needed to. I was missing my children, my lost childhood and there were so many ghosts I needed to bury. Perhaps this was the answer. Maybe I'd been at war with the wrong guy all these years after all. But once again my hopes were shattered and I fell to earth with a crash.

I was sitting in my cell one afternoon when there was a knock on the door. It was a couple of guys I knew, Jack and Sandy, asking me if I wanted to share a joint with them. I agreed. We smoked together and pretty soon another three guys came in. This wasn't an unusual occurrence. We often used to sit together and get stoned. What I didn't notice, however, was that I was smoking a lot more than they were. Jack asked me how old I was. I told him I was twenty-four. Then he asked if I missed my wife. Automatically I was alarmed. My hand went to my blade, but I wasn't quick enough. Two of them grabbed me. Bloody fool, I thought, they're going to nick my dope and tobacco; still I had more around the prison. I tried to get loose but five to one are not good odds and I was no Bruce Lee, worse luck. I couldn't make too much noise or the screws would've been alerted and I had quite a large chunk of dope in my cell.

The beds in prison have metal frames and they tied my hands over my head and to the bed frame. Then two of them sat on my legs, the others gagged me. I lay there waiting for them to look for my dope and tobacco, but they didn't. They were just whispering to each other and laughing. I wondered what the joke was. Then Jack asked if I remembered Alan. Alan was a guy who pestered me in the showers, one of the queens I have mentioned. I had got annoyed when he wouldn't leave me alone and stabbed him. I thought, oh well, they're going to cut me, could be worse. Jack signalled to the two on my legs. They got up and started to rip my shorts off. My mind went blank and I froze.

Then Jack was raping me. My mind went back to Gino and the bike. I wouldn't scream or even move, then perhaps they would go away. They didn't. They all took turns. They burned me with matches and cigarettes to try to get me to do things I cannot bring myself to write about. How long it went on I don't know; I just looked round and they were gone.

I tried to sit up but the pain doubled me over. I managed to swing my legs off the bed – at least they'd untied me. I rolled a joint and inhaled deeply. I couldn't think. I felt crushed. I looked across at the bars. I had to get out somehow. I couldn't stay in that cell. How long I sat there I don't know. What I did know, though, was that I had to pay them back. I could not let it go or every queen in the prison would be after me. Plus I needed revenge. Jack was the leader; he would be first, then the others.

I had been given a job in the gardens, so it was very easy for me to make my way around the prison. Jack worked in the kitchen and one of his jobs was to empty the rubbish. There were huge bins surrounded by a brick wall so I waited behind the bins. Needless to say, Jack spent quite some time in hospital afterwards.

Peter Timms got wind of something going on. He thought it was drug-related, so I was put in the block and the others were shipped out to other prisons.

My time in the block gave me time to think – something I needed to do. I believed at the time that Peter knew what had happened to me. He called me in to see him and said he was ninety-nine per cent certain that it was me who had nearly killed Jack but he didn't have proof.

When I met Peter many years later, after he'd become

a church minister, he asked me if he had been right. I told him he had been right. When he found out why I'd done it, however, he was aghast. He told Joanne that he'd had no idea; he had really believed it was drug-related. As I was so heavily involved in drugs it's easy to see why he came to that conclusion.

I really spent time thinking. Peter told me I could either change and move on or stay the same and spend the rest of my life in prison. He told me he would help me all he could. I had nothing to lose so I tried to change. Peter said he felt God could have a place in my life. I laughed, but deep down I wondered and somewhere within me I wanted to change any way I could.

I gave up drugs the hard way by going cold turkey in a strip cell. Everything I've ever done I've done the hard way. No easy way out for me. I started behaving myself and wasn't put on report again, so five and a half years after walking into prison I walked out. I was ready to try again.

I had a house, a wife, a new life. I was really prepared to try this time. I was even willing to forget my wrongful imprisonment. My life this time was going to be different.

I was home again. Everything seemed so big, so different. The world had changed. Because of the drug stupor I had been in I hadn't heard of a lot of the changes and it was a heck of a shock. Even Anne was different. She'd changed out of all recognition – more grown-up, I suppose. Was it going to be as easy as I thought? Or would I come crashing down again as I had so many times in the past?

12

I was back home again, yet I wasn't. The world had moved on while I'd been in prison, but it seemed as though I had stood still. Anne was a stranger. Although we were man and wife it was as if we'd met only briefly years before and we remembered each other, but only just.

Nothing was as I expected it to be. I managed to find work but as soon as they found out that I had been in prison I was shown the door. Powerful people from my past wanted me on a leash and they intended to put me on one any way they could. I was just as determined to stay free. I tried working for myself but things were not the same as they were before my prison term; doors that were once open were now closed to me. I was on my own; still I was going to make a go of it. I just had to keep on trying; things would improve.

Anne decided on a holiday – we would go to Great Yarmouth. It sounded just right, I'd always loved the coast, although it seemed that whenever we went she came back pregnant. We thought the break would be good for both of us. So off we set.

It was really enoyable and, as always, she did come back pregnant. We thought a child would help to fetch us together again. Anne tried really hard, but it was as if I was no longer capable of giving or receiving love. I was dead inside.

I thought I could put behind me all the bad things that had happened to me, but far from helping, Anne being pregnant made it worse. I was seeing my dead children everywhere. I'd been told that Karen had given birth to a little girl, but she was in America and I couldn't see or hold her. It was sending me crazy. I suppose it wouldn't have been so bad if I'd had someone to confide in, but I had no one. I wanted so much to tell Anne of the existence of my other child but I knew I never could. I even thought of going to America to find her, but there was no excuse I could give Anne for the trip, so I pushed it to one side and hoped it would go away. That's what I did regarding all my problems. Most of the time it worked but this time it didn't; it just got worse. Even now I've never seen my daughter, but I hope that one day I will.

Every time my problems had got worse in the past I had turned back to drugs. This time was no different. However, I convinced myself that I wasn't going to get hooked again; I would only take small amounts here and there just to see me through the bad times. What I didn't accept then was that I was a drug addict and even a tiny amount would set me off again.

With the drug-taking obviously came crime; drugs were not cheap and it was the only way to pay for them. This time, however, I went downhill much faster. Within a week I was as bad an addict as I had been before. The one difference was that now I needed more to sustain me; the old amounts were not enough. My willingness to commit violence increased, the hallucinations came back and I was finding it hard to keep track of reality.

I plotted to kill a man, the man I held responsible for

sending me to prison. In fact he was guilty but that was no reason to kill him. I convinced myself it was. I got myself a gun and waited for him for a whole week. Finally I spotted him. I lined the gun up on him and began to squeeze the trigger. Bastard, I thought, you're dead. But try as I might I could not fire that gun. I have never used so much effort in my life before as I did in those few seconds. I just couldn't do it. It was as if something or someone stopped me. I even put the gun into my own mouth but still I could not pull that trigger. I felt such a failure, as if someone had kicked all the wind out of me. I drove to Tower Bridge and tossed the gun into the water. If only I could've followed it but I knew I couldn't do that either. I was on an endless train and I couldn't get off, at least not until the journey's end. I had to wait until the end whenever that would be. This unseen God had once again stopped me. Why? Why would He not let me kill that guy or myself?

I had to wait another seventeen years to find the answer. Now I thank God that He did stop me.

Then came another blow. I was working, driving a van in Smithfield meat market in London's East End. I was managing to get by – just. Anne was getting ready for the birth of our next child and also holding down a full-time job, when my mother had a stroke. I wasn't really worried. She was a tough old girl, I thought, who would outlast all of us. But she didn't. I came home from work one day to be told by Anne that she had died early that morning.

It was a tremendous blow to me. I'd lost children, close friends, my dad – but my mum was different. She was the only friend I had, or that's how I felt. I didn't realize how much she had meant to me until then. I loved her, yet I'd not had the chance to tell her about all that had happened to me. Now I never would.

I was glad when the funeral was over because now I could break away. I was determined to make some money, leave the country and start again. I was working out all these different schemes, and at the same time getting involved in burglaries and a few robberies. I also started running drugs again. But as soon as I made money I spent it again. I seemed to be getting nowhere fast.

Then it all came to a stop. I was arrested again. This time the charge was aggravated burglary and rape. I convinced myself that I'd been fitted up again. I even convinced myself that the girl was involved in the conspiracy to get me. I wasn't going to lie down to this one. I was going to fight them all the way. It got me nowhere. I was found guilty and sentenced to five years.

It took me a few years to work out that I had not been fitted up this time. This time I was guilty. I had committed the one crime I swore I would never do. I had become as bad as the people who had raped me.

I made excuses for myself and the crime I'd committed when in reality I had no excuse. Nor do I offer one now. I was and am guilty. I could say sorry for what I did, but that wouldn't compensate her. I raped her then put her through the ordeal of a trial when there was no need for one. There is nothing I can say that can change that other than at that time it wasn't her I was fighting, it was the ghosts from my past and we all know we can't fight ghosts, don't we?

My wife said she'd had enough. She couldn't take any more and she decided to end our marriage. I wanted to keep it going for the sake of the child she was carrying. You may think that was a selfish reason. You'd be right, it was. But after the loss of my other children I could not let go. I would fight for my child any way I could. He was mine. Anne was just a vessel who was carrying it. She had nothing else to do with it as far as I was concerned. She couldn't protect it, only I could do that. How I would do it I didn't know. I would sort that out later.

I was fighting a charge of rape, a charge I could go away for for a very long time, but this took second place. The only thing that mattered was my unborn child.

Time went on and eventually I was told my wife had given birth to a boy and all was well. A few weeks later I received a letter with some photos of him. Anne told me she had called him James. I wasn't asked about that; I was just told. Looking back, I suppose my indignant attitude could be called unjustified. I hadn't treated her right and she was going through divorce proceedings. But at the time it really annoyed me and made me very bitter towards her. I decided I wasn't going to let her get away with it. She wasn't going to leave me out of the picture that easily. After all I was his father and she was the one who was ending our marriage, wasn't she? I would fight her just as I had fought everybody else. I began to see all the women as being the same and over the weeks the girl I had raped and my wife became one and the same person. I was going to destroy her any way I could. This was to lead to me nearly being killed.

I was going a bit crazy, ranting and raving. I was completely out of control. I didn't eat or drink anything for sixteen days and I was raving about all the things that had happened to me as a child. By now I was in the hospital in Brixton prison which was full of crazy people, so you might think nobody would take any notice of me. But as I was mentioning in my ravings the names of very powerful and well-known people, somebody did take notice. I began to realize that I was being given acid and with that came the knowledge that a prison officer was trying to kill me. Another inmate who was on a murder charge told me that this officer had asked him to stab me and that the officer would take good care of him for doing it. Ravings of a crazy man you may think, but I had heard of this kind of thing before.

My brothers John and Bill came in to see me and I told them my fears. John was really worried about me and asked if he got it sorted out would I start eating again. I promised him I would. My brother Bill went to the police and a policeman came in to see me. We did a trade. I gave him information about drugs and he warned the prison officer that if anything happened to me he would be investigated for murder along with the governor whose care I was in. I was moved to a single cell after the policeman left.

Around midnight that night, the cell door started to open. I shouted that I hadn't taken my medication and that the first one through the door would be dead. I heard a voice I recognized as the prison officer's telling me he could wait. I told him I could wait too and I would. He was out shopping the next day when a friend of mine walked up to him and warned him that if he didn't lay off me he would be the dead one.

He asked me for a truce. I told him I agreed but only because I was in prison. He didn't come near me again.

The prison doctor tried to convince me that it was all in my mind, but he never did succeed.

As I'd helped the police over a drugs enquiry, I had to spend the rest of my term in special protection. I was sent to a special unit in Albany prison on the Isle of Wight and there I stayed for most of my sentence. The good thing about it was that I met up with an old mate, Joe, my Christian friend from Maidstone.

My divorce papers were served on me, so it was over, I was a free agent. Only in a manner of speaking, that is. If the locked doors, cameras and walls were taken away I would be free. I was still a dad and fighting to see my son. I had been given access to see him. The trouble was they wouldn't let me out and Anne wouldn't bring him in. It was like being given an ice cream and told not to lick it. I was a dad in name only and it was sending me crazy. Everything I tried came to nothing. I decided that when I left prison I would kill Anne. I used to lie in my cell and think up ways of doing away with her, then my son and I would ride off into the sunset to live happily ever after. Wonderful thing, our imagination; in there things always come out right. The trouble is in the real world our dreams do not always come true.

Joe was coming on to me really strong about this guy called Jesus and he was starting to make me think maybe he was right and I was wrong. You see, ever since I first went to prison people had seemed to fall into my path. Brian, a vicar in a London prison, gave me doubts, Peter Timms in Maidstone really rocked my boat, Joe in here and also a Methodist minister who was such a nice guy. Looking back now it was as if I had gone behind closed doors and through all these people God had put in my way He was slowly opening those doors to let the light in. I was also in the future to meet a young Christian girl called Joanne. She was going not only to let light in, she was going to cause such an explosion in me I would never be the same again.

I was working in the workshop where we had to cut the tags off kettle feet. You may ask what on earth I'm talking about. Well, the little plastic feet that go onto kettles have little wings on them when they come out of the mould. It was our job to cut these wings off. Very demanding work it was that needed a lot of concentration and we would work away happily, snipping and cutting. It really did prepare us for life outside prison.

I was working away quite happily when I was told I had a governor's call up. I thought it might have something to do with my son James as I was still fighting to see him. I walked into the governor's office.

"Name and number to the governor," the officer said.

I as always pressed my self-destruct button. "Why?" I asked. "Have you forgotten it or lost it, guv?"

The governor smiled. "Never mind, Angus."

Oh, no, I thought, it must be serious. He called me Angus. He now had my full attention. He informed me that I had been given nine weeks' parole and I would be released on 19 March 1983.

I laughed. "Don't muck about, guv. What do you really want?"

He assured me it was true and that he was as amazed as I was. It was on one condition though. Here's the catch, I thought. What would they want in return? He told me I would have to go into a drug rehabilitation programme at Phoenix House as a condition of licence. I told him I had not taken drugs for over two years. He told me to think about it and to come back in an hour. Wow, that really gave me a long time to debate it, didn't it?

I decided to accept their nine weeks. Some people are given two or three years' licence. What do I get? A lousy nine weeks. Still, better nine weeks out there than in here, I thought.

I told Joe what had happened over our evening meal and he reminded me that God spoke to him. I told him to keep taking the pills. He was the one person who wouldn't get angry, even though many times I would take the mick. It was most irritating: he was always happy. It got to me and I suppose I envied him. He smiled, then proceeded to tell me what God had told him. He said that within a year of being released I would meet a girl of eighteen called Joanne and we would get married. I told him he was crazy. I'd just been divorced. I wasn't going to go through all that again. He told me she would have blue eyes and went on to describe her. He's got a lovely imagination, I thought – eighteen, sexy blue eyes. Wow if I had a girl like that I'd be made up, wouldn't I?

The thing was he was right, especially about the eyes. Boy was she gorgeous. When I met Joanne, it didn't hit me straight away that this was the girl Joe had been talking about, but when it did it had a profound effect on me.

13

It was coming up for Christmas 1982. I was moved to Maidstone prison to prepare me for my release.

Before I knew where I was it was the night before my release. I had applied for home leave and was turned down. They said I might not return. I would've laughed if it hadn't been so pathetic – nine weeks to go before the end of my sentence and they were worried I might not return. I didn't sleep that night. I couldn't wait for the morning to come but it came sooner than I expected.

I had cleared out my cell the night before. I was going out with nothing. I had even given away my radio. Everything had gone. All I had was the clothes I stood up in. I was drug-free and had been for nearly two years, the longest I'd gone since I was seven years old. I was still fighting to see my son and still fighting to get the 1974 conviction overturned, and not getting anywhere. But I felt a strange peace as if for once everything was going to work out. I was full of optimism for the future. My conviction would be quashed; I would get to see my son – when I didn't know – but I wasn't bothered.

I walked out through the gates and turned to watch them close behind me. I felt different this time. I was older but I knew that wasn't it. It was as if I wasn't alone. Stupid, I thought. I shook myself. Of course I'm alone. Nobody came to meet me – I hadn't even told anyone. I was alone, wasn't I?

I made my way to the station for my train journey to London. I was going home. I had no home and yet I felt I did. After a hectic train journey I arrived back in London. The rush hour takes a bit of getting used to for most people, but after a few years in prison it was like a madhouse. I didn't know if my nerves could stand it.

I made my way to my sister's house where she greeted me with "You must be hungry". It was as if I hadn't been away – well that's my sister. After eating I told her and her husband Chick that I had to go to a drug treatment centre. Chick asked me if that was what I wanted and I told him I wasn't sure. He was more like a dad than a brother-in-law and I had told him more about my past than I had anyone. Yet he never betrayed that trust I'd put in him. He was to die a short time later and I still miss him.

We all went for a drink and Chick told me he didn't think that the drug treatment centre would do me a lot of good. He thought I needed help to sort out all the things I had gone through and to come to terms with them. He was right in a way.

I left them and went to Phoenix House. They wouldn't accept me because I had been drinking so I told them to suit themselves and left. I then visited other members of my family and ended up getting drunk with one of my brothers. So ended my first day of freedom.

The next day I made my way back to Phoenix House, sober this time. It was not a great success. As I've said, I had already been away from the drug scene for two years while all the other people there had just started to come off. They taught me how to express my anger but not how to control it. I had a tremendous amount of anger inside me and they showed me how to let it loose. They told me I might think it was OK to tell someone to piss off, but in the normal world it isn't acceptable. Others may find this kind of therapy helpful; it just wasn't for me. I was looking for something else. I didn't know what, but something. I told my parole officer. He wasn't pleased. You see, because it was a condition of my release that I attend this place, by not going they could easily recall me to serve the rest of my sentence. But in the end he agreed to go along with me. I was relieved as I didn't particularly want to go back to prison to serve my last five weeks.

I was like a blind man in a strange room groping around trying to find the door. I was really desperate to change but I just did not know how. I managed to get a job as a night chef. I knew nothing about the job but I convinced my employers that I did. It only paid forty pounds a week but it was better than unemployment money. I moved in with my brother Bill who had a small two-bedroomed flat in Mottingham, a small town in southeast London near Eltham.

I finally managed to get a place of my own. It was only a tiny two-bedroomed flat on the Downham Estate in Catford right opposite the cemetery, but I liked it. I applied for a job in a very large electrical company and was very surprised when I got it.

I was enjoying my new-found freedom. I was working for a living. No drugs, no crime, no prostitution. I was drinking, though, but to my way of thinking I was working hard and entitled to that. I had also given up the idea of killing my ex-wife and I put my son on hold.

The job was going well. I was earning over three hundred pounds a week – more money than I'd seen in a long time. Needless to say I squandered it. Every night there was a different girl if I wanted one and I felt that life was good. I was enjoying myself. The police were being a bit of a pest but I thought that if I ignored them they would go away, or at least I hoped they would.

I started having trouble with one of the foremen at work. He didn't like "jailbirds" and he had been trying to get the job for his son. We had a few disagreements then I found out that he was having an affair with a young lady in the office. I had become very arrogant so I went out of my way to gain her attention. He caught us one day and swore he and his son would get me. I laughed and told him that if his son was as big a wimp as his dad then I wouldn't have a lot to worry about. I told him to get lost or he would get hurt. I walked out and laughed. I was still quite a pig at times and that self-destruct button hadn't been disabled. I still pressed it at times.

I went in to work the next morning and as I walked through the door I felt a blow that sent me staggering forward. The part of me that was the street kid took over and both men landed up with a few broken bones. I was suspended pending an enquiry. I picked up my pay and headed for the pub. It was no big deal, or so I thought. As usual it wasn't my fault, it was someone else's, so I drowned my sorrows and pitied myself.

The next night my brother and I went to a local pub as we always did in the evenings. We were sitting drinking when I noticed a young girl up at the bar. I thought she was about seventeen and really lovely. When she smiled her whole face seemed to light up. She seemed so happy and carefree, so full of fun; she really had a strange effect on me. I got her attention and she came over smiling, bringing a friend. She asked if she might help me. Not half, I thought. She sat down and introduced herself as Joanne, Jo for short. She told me her friend's name but I didn't hear it – I had eyes and ears for her only – the rest of the world had disappeared as far as I was concerned. I had never enjoyed myself or laughed so much in my life as I did that evening. It was as if we had known each other all our lives and not just a few hours. I could've stayed there forever just listening to her voice, her laugh, and each time she touched my hand or cheek an electrical charge seemed to surge through my body. I couldn't understand this; it had never happened to me before. I had never felt such strong emotions for anyone and it confused the life out of me.

She told me she would be late home. I asked how late. She said she was supposed to be home at midnight and it was now approaching two in the morning. She said her parents would go crazy. I asked if her father was a big guy and she told me he was bigger than me. He was and so was her mother; we could not have been serious if we'd tried.

We approached her parents' house. Jo wanted me to make a good impression, so she told me to watch what I said and I agreed. A bit daft, really, asking me that. After all, she was already nearly two hours late home; you couldn't give more of a bad impression if you tried. Her mother opened the front door.

"Hi, Mum, hi, Dad, my name's Gus," I said. Not a very good start I thought to myself. Her mother wasn't impressed at all. Not only was this man someone she'd never met before but he was bringing her daughter home two hours late and he was also the worse for drink.

Her parents decided to be polite for their daughter's sake and greeted me. After the introductions I was asked if I wanted a cup of coffee and we sat down in the kitchen. Then came the questions, like where had we been and what had we been doing? I opened my mouth to speak. Jo looked at me as if to say, "You do." I closed my mouth again deciding that silence was the best policy. The questions went on for what seemed like hours but they didn't get any answers out of us. In the end they gave up and left the kitchen, leaving us on our own. Jo flung her arms around me trying hard not to laugh too loud – it did seem funny to us at the time.

We spent the next hour talking, getting to know each other. Then her father came back and announced that it was half past three and they were waiting to go to bed. We walked out to the front gate and carried on our conversation.

She told me it would be very easy for her to fall in love with me. I felt exactly the same. The mood was very romantic. We exchanged cigarettes and she took my lighter off me to light them. I lowered my head and whoosh, the flame went right up my nose. Instead of losing my temper as I normally did, I burst out laughing. So did she. Our romantic mood was broken by a voice from the darkness.

"Do you intend staying out there all night, Joanne?"

Jo took my hand and whispered, "I wish I could." I was in agreement with her and we carried on talking. It wasn't that we deliberately ignored her parents but we just didn't want to say goodnight to each other. It was as though we'd been searching for each other for years and now we'd found one another we didn't want to let go.

There was that voice again, "Joanne, it's nearly a quarter past four; if you don't come in I'll lock the door."

That was our cue to say goodnight. I'd already created a bad impression and I didn't want to make it any worse than it was. We really hated saying goodbye that night, but we did it, we had no choice. We arranged before I went to meet the following night. We hadn't even left each other and already I was wishing for the next night to come.

Walking home that night I realized just how vulnerable I was. I was at the mercy of a world I knew nothing about. The normal world was as alien to me as Earth would be to a Martian. How could I be normal? I'd spent eight years in the world of prison and another twenty in the company of porn makers and prostitutes. How was I to speak and behave? That I didn't know but I was hoping to find out.

I'd told Jo that I'd been in prison, but not why. I couldn't. I wanted to see her again and I thought that if I told her then she wouldn't want to see me. I should've picked up her lead, though, when she told me that it didn't matter to her what I'd done. It was past and as long as I treated her right she wasn't bothered. I suppose I wanted her to get to know me, the personality first rather than what other people branded me. I had told her other things about me, though, that I'd been married and it hadn't worked out. She wasn't jealous or put off by anything I told her and her reaction was one of interest only. She had wanted to get to know me. She was the first woman I knew that was interested in me and not in what she could get out of me. Even so, I didn't know whether she would wish to see me again. I was so unsure of myself, so nervous. Had I told her too soon? Would she be put off? These were questions that I would only have the answers to the following night, so I would have to wait. That night I prayed that she would meet me again and I recognized that strange feeling that I had felt for my children, that feeling of love. But how could I? I'd only just met her. Yet I knew that I did.

I didn't sleep at all that night, I was too nervous. The following day I was on edge from the time I got up until the evening. She'd turn up, she was different, special, she wouldn't let me down. The evening came. I'd arranged to meet her in the same pub. I'd already worked the evening out. When she arrived we would go on somewhere else, just the two of us. My brother had come along with me so we ordered a drink and waited, and waited. It got later and later and she didn't turn up. To say I was hurt was an understatement. It felt as if someone had kicked me in the guts to put it bluntly. But I couldn't understand that because I'd never been bothered before. If a girl had stood me up in the past I'd just shrugged and found another one. With Jo it was different; I was really gutted. I thought I'd blown it, frightened her off. Then I started to get angry. I'll fix her, I thought.

I made my way to her parents' house. They informed me that Jo was asleep so I told them that she was supposed to meet me that night. Her father told me she'd changed her mind. I didn't believe him. I stood there arguing for a while until I realized she wasn't going to appear and then left. I knew she was awake. I could just feel it but I knew I wasn't going to get anywhere that night, so I went home.

I tried twice more to see her at her parents' house but didn't succeed. I couldn't understand it. My friend Joe from prison had told me about this girl. I was sure now it was the same one because he'd described her perfectly and here she was. So why was she giving me the brush-off? I was really confused. I was sure this was the girl for me. I couldn't get her out of my mind, so what was this guy called God playing at?

I started to drink heavily to try and stop thinking about her, but it didn't work. I tried going out with other women but everyone reminded me of her so I gave that up and concentrated on trying to forget her. But there was a part of me that still wanted to see her again so I started praying for her to come back to me, hoping that I would be answered, not even knowing if I had been heard. I started to get involved in fights. I was bad-tempered the whole time. The firm I had been working for decided they could take me back but only if I went on a management training course in Wales. It would've meant leaving Jo. Although I wasn't with her I had to stay near her, so I refused.

A couple of weeks after meeting Jo I was taken seriously ill and rushed into hospital with a burst duodenal ulcer – it's an occupational hazard for people who have been in prison. I realized there was a chance I could die, but for the first time in my life I wanted to live. I'd found Joanne and I didn't want to lose her now. My brother asked me if I wanted him to fetch her, thinking that would help me improve. I told him that if he did I would discharge myself. She had to come because she wanted to, not out of pity or because she felt she had to. I really prayed. I asked God to make me well and to give me back this girl. That night I slept for the first time.

I awoke the next morning and there was no pain, no discomfort. I didn't tell the doctors about my prayers. I just got dressed and left. God had healed me, I thought. The doctors told me I would kill myself. But I knew best – after all what did they know? I had to get back to Eltham for I felt sure that when I walked along Joanne's road she would be there at her gate waiting for me. Needless to say she wasn't.

I was bitterly disappointed. I felt God was laughing at me. I decided that if God was having some fun then so would I and promptly went and got drunk.

I didn't know at the time that God *was* there for me. He always had been. At the worst times in my life – the death of my children, when I nearly died myself as a child, shattered by pain or grief – whatever it was – I never felt alone. It was as if someone was there with me, waiting to pick me up and carrying me through. Then I would go back behind my doors again and close them and I would be alone again.

That night my brother and I went for a drink in the same pub where I'd met Jo. At the end of the evening we went to buy a kebab. As we entered the shop I heard someone call my name. At first I thought it was a young guy I'd upset, so I told my brother to get the kebab and I would be along later after knocking this person out. I wanted a row with someone and this guy would do. As I got halfway across the road I recognized this guy as being Joanne. She had been waiting for me for quite some time and boy was she mad. I walked over to give her a hug and she pushed me away. I asked her what was wrong. Reading between the lines, she seemed to me to be very lonely and when I didn't make a determined play for her felt very left out. I told her I'd been in hospital. She didn't believe me. I called my brother over so that he could tell her. As she listened to him she flung her arms around me and apologized. My brother, totally forgotten, walked away.

Jo saw that I'd lost a lot of weight – by now I only weighed six stone and was like a bag of bones. She told me she would never leave me again. I heard these words but I didn't take them in. I'd heard them so many times before from others. Was this another empty promise? She didn't know much about me. Would it mean nothing when she *did* know and would she drop me like a hot brick? I couldn't trust her. I couldn't trust anyone. To be let down once is easy to get over but I'd been let down hundreds of times.

I'd never told anyone about the shame, the dirtiness I felt from the age of seven. Because of this I had a compulsion for washing. The dirt on the outside became the dirt I felt on the inside and I wanted to cleanse myself of it. My defences had been up for years and I'd been quite happy for that to continue, but now I felt vulnerable. Deep inside myself I knew Jo was the key but could I let her unlock these doors? My defences had been my life. I'd been used to standing alone and fighting my own battles. When the doors were opened, would Jo be strong enough to fight them for me or would those doors close again, crushing us both? I was frightened, not only for me but also for her. What would the future hold for us both?

For the first time in my life I felt an overwhelming

tiredness as though I needed someone else to lean on. But would Jo be able to prop me up? Reflecting back, the answer to that was no, but she showed me someone who would.

14

We met the following day and went to my brother's flat. There Jo told me a bit more about herself. She asked me not to laugh and then confirmed what Joe in prison had told me. She was a Christian. I did laugh, but not in a mocking way. I told her that I'd been friends with a Christian for years and explained what Joe had told me. Jo was delighted but she wouldn't tell me why. She later said that what I'd told her was an answer to a prayer. She'd always wanted someone like me, a lost cause, but she didn't realize at first just how lost I was. She knew, however, that Jesus had come for people such as me. He didn't give up, so neither would she. Jo was very young in her faith, and I hadn't even begun, so we had a great deal to learn.

It was as if Joanne and I were in a race; within three months of meeting we were married. Our first few months were peaceful and happy. I couldn't believe she was mine. I was so happy, but could I love? It would seem so. I just hoped the past was gone, behind me. The trouble was it would just not go away completely. Try as I did, it always seemed to come back.

Jo was drinking quite heavily as was I, so there wasn't a lot of conflict between us. She found she was pregnant and a miscarriage threatened at three months. After this she refused to drink and began asking me questions about my life.

By this time we were living on our own in our little flat but the questions became too much for me. I could disappear to have a drink but she was always there when I came back, probing, wanting answers, answers that I couldn't give her. Then I found my solution. We were broken into and I was attacked. It gave me an excuse for us to move out. I said I didn't feel Jo was safe staying on there, being seven months pregnant, in case the intruders came back. Jo was reluctant, saying she could take care of herself. I reminded her that it wasn't only herself she had to think of. She also had to think about our unborn child. I manipulated her and the situation to get what I wanted, which was to be surrounded by other people so that the questions would stop. I led her around to my way of thinking and we moved in with her parents. It gave me the perfect answer. Whenever Jo probed me about my life I used it against her. Her parents would become involved and an argument would begin, which would deflect her from the real issue. I then had an excuse to storm out of the house and get drunk and I wouldn't have to answer those questions. It worked for a time but then our new addition arrived – our son John was born.

In giving birth to our son it seemed as though Jo had also given birth to herself. She went into hospital a girl and came out a woman who seemed so sure of the direction her life was going to take, and she was determined she was going to take me down the same road. As far as she was concerned there was nothing I couldn't achieve. I wasn't so sure. She decided that we needed a place of our own. The arguments were getting worse and were beginning to pull us down. I had to get out. All relationships like this are a strain but this one had the added complication of my stubbornness and selfishness.

As a result of our application to the council, we were given a two-bedroomed town house. We were delighted with it. It was on one of the worst estates in the area – a typical concrete jungle. It was the type of estate I liked with plenty of dope and drink available. What more could a man like me ask for? By this time Jo's brother and I had introduced her to dope and we were spending the majority of our money on it. Our life consisted of getting stoned, listening to music and making love. You see, when I was in prison most of my time had been spent this way. I didn't have to face up to my problems. I could hide them away. The trouble was Jo was in my self-imposed prison.

One of the reasons I didn't tell her about my life was that society could accept women being raped, even a child, but a man – no way. It's not macho to be raped, is it? A girl gets sympathy, a boy gets told to pull himself together. There is also the point that if a man rapes a boy then he could well be homosexual. This attitude causes so many problems to the victim. He then starts to ask himself if *he* is a homosexual. If the rape is by a woman then he is told he is lucky and not to moan about it. The trouble is rape has no boundaries; whether a male or a female has been forced into sex the emotional problems are the same.

Everything had been going well at first and I was hardly drinking. It seemed as though I had left my problems behind me. This was to be short-lived, though, and they came back with a vengeance. My reasoning for getting Jo on to smoking cannabis was to stop her asking questions. It didn't. It only led her to ask more. I'd tried drink, I'd tried dope, but nothing seemed to sidetrack her from this guy she called Jesus. Not only did she tell me He was the most important thing in her life, but He was also directing her questions. As she pointed out quite happily, they'd nailed Him to a cross and it hadn't stopped Him. I couldn't stop her. She even told me she would give her life for me if the need arose. Her sincerity shocked me – she had such faith in Jesus. She pointed out to me that I would never understand her attitude until I'd experienced Jesus for myself.

She didn't behave like most people. When drugs are introduced they take over completely; drug-takers can't think or act normally. But Jo would act more than normal; her insight into things was heightened. She would pick up on things a lot quicker, grab hold of them and wouldn't let go. I couldn't win. I'd tried to stop the questions but only succeeded in making them worse. Then one night she took the bull by the horns and demanded to know what had happened to me. I got angry and all the hurt and pain of my past seemed to spew out. Far from leaping up and packing her bags, Jo really understood and comforted me. She told me the only way forward was to bury the past and talk about the hurt.

After this Jo took a more positive attitude to her Christianity and battered my eardrums constantly about Jesus. Christian records would be played and when I asked questions she would take great delight in answering them. I told her very angrily one night of an incident in prison. I was being beaten by some prison officers when the vicar arrived. I called out to him for help but he ignored my cries and left. He visited me a few days after the event and I informed him that he was just a screw with a dog collar. He responded by saying that he wasn't, he was a man of God. I asked him if God would've done what he did and his reply was, "You must have deserved it." I told him I supposed he was right – my only crime was to swear at an officer. He told me the officers had to keep order and anyway he couldn't do anything because he'd signed the Official Secrets Act.

After this, as you can imagine, my impression of Christians was not a good one. This was only one incident. There were many others. They reflected on only a small proportion of chaplains. The majority do their job very well. It made Jo's job harder that I saw all Christians as hypocrites. But she shot this idea down in flames. Gradually this girl was winning. I was even starting to like the Rock Gospel Show that she watched on TV.

Looking back, the war I'd declared on God was coming to an end. It had been a war on one side only in which I was the only aggressor. Through Jo He was signing the peace treaty after a war He hadn't started. He was pulling me towards Him but I was unsure if that's what I really wanted – until one day.

We'd had an argument about, need I say, Christianity. Jo had kept me awake until the early hours of the morning and yet again I'd lost. Next day I was in a thoroughly bad mood and just waiting to belt someone, so I made an excuse to go out. My intention was to drive to the nearest pub and get sozzled. I found that the end of our road was blocked by a camper van. On the rear of the van was a large sign proclaiming Jesus's love. I thought to myself, I can't get away from these

Christians, what with her all night and now this. I opened my window and shouted some obscenities. The driver leaned out of his window and told me that Jesus loved me, then drove off.

I asked myself in a mocking tone, "Do you love me, Jesus?" I was very surprised to hear a voice stating that yes, He did love me. I hadn't even been to the pub and already I was hearing voices. I wondered if I was having another breakdown. If I was then I knew I couldn't handle it, so I made my way to the pub. God intervened again. I felt that a voice inside me was saying, "No, not this time."

Although I would not admit it to myself, the bombardment of Christianity I'd received from Jo had a slight effect on me but her love and forgiveness totally threw me. I would push her to the limit at times and she always forgave me. No matter what I did or said, she carried on loving me and that affected me far more than any talking. I knew God was offering me a choice.

Stupid as it may seem I remained at that pub for nearly six hours and try as I might I couldn't touch the pint I had ordered. It remained in front of me the whole time. I felt like a man who was drowning and my whole life seemed to pass before me in slow motion. I had come full circle. I realized for the first time that I did have emotions, I did care. I voiced out loud, "If you want me, God, I'll come and meet you." I was still undecided. As far as I was concerned God didn't speak to people, especially people like me. I felt I was sliding back into the pit of drug addiction and despair and I didn't want to put my wife Jo and John through that. For once I would be noble. I would not only put them first, I would also confront her God. I decided that the only course open to me was death. If Jo was right I would meet my tormentor face to face and demand answers.

This time there would be no mistakes. I got into my car and took it onto a dual carriageway. The road seemed strangely empty as if for once this God was making it easy for me. I accelerated to over a hundred miles an hour, took my hands off the wheel and closed my eyes. There was an eerie silence. I had not felt an impact nor could I hear the engine. I thought, so this is death. I felt a strange peace and wellbeing, so I opened my eyes. There in front of me were not the pearly gates nor angels with harps, but the dual carriageway. The car was parked perfectly at the side of the road. There were no skid marks, no broken glass, not even a dented lamppost. I was totally freaked. What was happening to me? Then I heard this voice again. This time I instantly recognized it. It told me to go home. Who was I to argue? I did as I was told. I don't remember going home, but I know I got there. Suddenly Jo was there in front of me. She started to read me the riot act for being out all day without even a phone call, then stopped.

"What has happened to you?" she asked. "You look like an old man."

Believe me, I felt like one. I felt an overwhelming panic. I realized I was dying and told her as much. She agreed. Then she said something that she never had before.

"You know, there's only one person who can help you now."

"Yeah, Jesus," I replied.

Her mouth fell open. "Are you saying what I think you're saying? You want Jesus in your life?" I just nodded. I don't know what made her do it, but she ran past me into the kitchen. There she picked up the phone and spoke to her friend Terry in Ramsgate. He invited us to go down there next day.

In Ramsgate I invited Jesus into my life and believe me, this was no ordinary conversion. In the room with me were my wife and three other people. Each of them had been Christians for many years and none of them had felt God's power as strongly as they did that day. It seemed as though the whole of heaven was rejoicing and I honestly believed that this is what happened to everyone. Jo, who at the time was not living her life the way God wanted her to, felt the power as much as the others.

I became a new person then and there. The back trouble that had plagued me for years completely vanished. Before that day I'd found it hard even to pick my son up. Now I was on the cliffs with him on my shoulders and I didn't even realize it until Jo warned me that I might damage it. I replied, "My back is no longer damaged; it has been healed." From that day to this I've had no more problems with it.

Over the next few months the change in me continued. My bad language ceased, my drinking stopped completely and I no longer took or even wanted any drugs. Things were really happening fast. People started to hear about me and I was invited to talk at meetings and speak about my life. But my life wasn't an open book; there were still things that I was ashamed of, things I didn't want anyone to know about except Jo. I left huge chunks out hoping they would go away. Christians were telling me that my past life was dead, that I was a new creation. It was true, I was. But as a new creation, I had to deal with the whole of my old life and not just parts. When I approached other established Christians they told me to give it all back to God and He would deal with it. Jo was also telling me to give the whole of my life story to God. The trouble was — could I? I now know I needed more help of the human kind in the form of counselling. My emotions were in tatters. I'd been torn apart and put back together again. I'd been shown a new life but not how to cope with it.

I was treated as a celebrity. Miracles followed me around wherever I went. God was healing, setting people free. He was using *me*. Established Christians didn't know what to do with me. I seemed to have shot past most of them. People were approaching me when they had problems hoping that I could sort them out. In many cases I did, but I was just a baby. I'd only been a Christian a very short while and in being thrust into the limelight like this it was obvious that something had to give.

Since I was a child I had wanted to live by the coast. After meeting Jo's friends in Ramsgate I decided I wanted to live there as well. So we took up residence in Margate. I wanted to leave all my problems behind wrapped up in a little suitcase, and for a time I did. God still used me after we moved, but things began to go wrong. I was portraying change on the surface but more and more the spirit that spoke to me was more out of a bottle than the Bible.

The past I'd tried to leave in London came back. We'd had a problem with the Social Services while we were still in London. They'd discovered my criminal record and decided to investigate. They seemed to take great delight in telling my wife the details of my 1974 conviction, possibly in the hope that she didn't know anything about it. They were greatly surprised to learn that not only did she know but that she had been told by a probation officer that he knew I'd been fitted up. They held a case conference and with the help and support of our GP decided there was no need to be concerned for our son. We were silly enough to think this was the end of it. We were to be proved wrong.

Over the next year we were to learn that the Social Services in Thanet had been informed about me and that was to be the start of a nightmare that we would have to endure. For me it was to be the final push that would break open the doors completely and I wasn't to know then that one day I would thank them.

I couldn't handle the pressure all this was putting on me and it finally came to a head with me turning to drugs as I had in the past. But the trouble was I wasn't the same person. The drugs totally blew my mind and resulted in an act of stupidity that was to cost me six months in prison.

This time it was different. I was no longer the hardened criminal. I was a wreck. Jo saw this as a great opportunity to get me the help I needed. She wrote to the prison psychiatrist setting out my problems and asking for help. The psychiatrist was greatly impressed by Jo's initiative. I had no choice. I couldn't exactly go anywhere, could I? I had to face up to reality.

My cell door opened one morning and a social worker called Heidi invited me to an open meeting. I saw it as a good excuse to get out of my cell for a while. How wrong I was. She started to have a go at me about the way I'd treated Jo. I got very angry and before I realized what was happening I was shouting, "Never mind other people. What about me?"

"What about you?" she screamed. "What makes you different?"

All of a sudden I was crying. All the hatred and pain was coming out like a torrent and I couldn't stop. Then Heidi was putting her arms around me, telling me I was safe. The doors were finally opening. It was to be the start of a very slow process. I was to have to face up not only to the crimes that had been committed against me, but to the horrendous crimes I had committed and take responsibility for them. It was to take those four months of counselling in prison to enable me to talk to other people about my problems but I would take another four years to sort them out.

During this time God used me to bring a lot of men in prison to Him. The prison chaplain asked my wife to tell me not to keep telling people about Jesus – he had nowhere to put them all.

Whilst in prison we had a visit from Archbishop Desmond Tutu and the outcome was that he invited me to visit him in Cape Town, which I hope to do in the future.

For those six months Jo never missed a visit and while on remand I could see her every day. Nothing stopped her from coming even though it would take her over an hour's travelling each way. This greatly impressed not only the officers but also the other prisoners. She always had time for other wives even though at the time she was coming to terms with her own childhood, which was very painful on its own without the problem of my predicament. She ran errands for other prisoners, arranging visits over the phone, dealing with their everyday problems. A lot of these men had been let down badly by women in the past so Jo's helpfulness and love restored their hope for future relationships. My wife is not a saint, at times she got depressed like anyone else but she refused to show it to anyone who might be hurt by it. She'd been hurt in the past and she didn't want to put anyone else through that hurt. But that's her story.

So came the time when I was released. Jo and I had been keeping a calendar, marking off each day until I went home. The day came and I was nervous. Was this closeness we felt going to continue or had we changed too much? My doubts, I soon realized, were unfounded. We were to become even closer.

I was to be released at seven fifteen in the morning and Jo was to be there when I came out. It would be the first time anybody would meet me and I wondered if this would herald a new era in my life.

All went well until they decided to let me out three quarters of an hour early – and I had no coat. This was November and cold. How could they do this to me? Little did I know things were also going wrong in Margate. Peter Timms was supposed to drive Jo to the prison but he had slept in. She didn't know that while she was phoning to get him out of bed, I was standing on the pavement freezing cold. The officer on the gate invited me in for a cup of coffee. I'd just spent six months in there and I certainly wasn't going back in! Just then a car appeared. It screeched to a halt. Even before it had completely stopped the door was opening and Jo came flying out. I thought she was going to crush me. Thank goodness – she'd bought my coat.

If you can imagine living on a desert island for six months, not even hearing the sound of a car then you will understand my fear. Normal driving I wouldn't have minded too much, but Peter, an ex-prison governor, drove like a getaway driver. Every now and again he would look over his shoulder and shout, "All right in the back?" I would manage to croak, "Yes" in a high-pitched voice. He told us happily that his wife was cooking us a celebration breakfast. I just prayed we would get there to eat it. Peter, I think you're a great driver, as long as you're at least a mile ahead of me.

As I had looked over my shoulder at the closing gates of the prison I knew the doors I'd closed so long ago were now open. I was no longer a hurt boy; I was learning how to be a man.

15

We were home and we marked off the last day on Jo's calendar together. It felt so good to be home at last. Our dog ran to greet me and as I hugged her, Jo's eyes and mine met. We didn't say a word – we didn't need to. We were only half a family – all we could hear was the ticking of the clock, something that was impossible when our little boy was around.

One battle was over but there was another one beginning. We cried silently, holding each other, both with our own memories of our son, but each with the same burning pain, the same emptiness inside. We were mother and father in name only. He'll be home soon, we promised each other, not knowing what lay in store for us or how long our fight would be. The elation of my arrival home was to be short-lived.

Before by short prison term the authorities had placed our son's name on the "at risk register", solely because of my past criminal convictions. I took it to mean that they suspected me of abuse, so when Jo visited me after my first court appearance and told me that she had sent him to her parents' house in London, I was pleased. It not only separated him from the pain my wife was going through, it also kept him safe from the long arm of the authorities. We believed they wouldn't be able to touch him there. As it turned out I couldn't have been more wrong. They considered that while he was in London, he wasn't "at risk" from me. The authorities held a case conference a couple of weeks before I was released and Jo was asked if she intended having me back into the family home. She replied yes and they informed her that our son would be better left where he was. Having as much knowledge of the legal system as the average person, she thought it would only take a few months to be sorted out before our son would be back home with us.

It came as a great shock when I was informed three days before my release and in a very cold way that my son had been made a ward of the court and that he wasn't to be removed from London until the court agreed. It seemed to me that they wanted a fight with my son in the middle and I wanted so much to oblige them. What this effectively meant was that the court now had overall responsibility for our son. We were not allowed to make any major decisions in his life. For example, we couldn't decide for ourselves the school we could send him to without the court's approval. We weren't allowed to take him on holiday out of the country. Hospital appointments had to be approved as well. We were no longer treated as his parents. It's a horrible feeling to have a child and yet not be allowed to decide his future.

You may wonder why this was such a shock. I was sitting in my cell that morning and I was really happy. Jo was coming in to see me; we were going to make plans for our future together; we were going to arrange for our son to come home, make a trip up to London and have a happy reunion. Then the door opened and I was told that I had a visitor. She's early, I thought. Good we'll have longer together. I was taken over to the visiting room. It was empty. First in, I thought, that's my Jo. I was shown into a private booth and I smiled to myself. That's nice of them, I thought, to make the last visit a private one.

My happiness turned to cold ice in the pit of my stomach when a social worker walked in. I didn't know what he was going to say but my senses told me it wouldn't be good. "Lord," I prayed, "please be with me. Let me not hurt this man."

He greeted me with a smile, this man who never smiled. It was a smile without warmth or feeling. He sat down and told me in such a gloating way that my son had been made a ward of court and all that entailed, that in fact I was officially no longer a father. I gripped my hands tightly under the table seeing him yet not seeing him. At that moment his face took on the many faces of all the people who had abused and tormented me down the years. Then I heard him ask from a long way off and his voice was filled with fear, "Do you understand what I'm telling you?"

I smiled. "You bastard." I started to rise. I would wipe him, all of them, from the face of the earth. Another voice spoke to me, calming me, a voice I loved and respected. Thank goodness for prayer. He was there with me. How could I fail Him? I turned and walked out, not seeing or hearing anything. Then Jo was there, holding me. How she got there I don't know but I know God's timing was perfect because I needed her at just that moment.

The trouble was that while I was in prison, I was so wrapped up in what was happening to me that I didn't fully realize the terrible pressure Jo had been put under to end our marriage. Members of her own family had tried to get her to leave me. I'd even asked her to leave me at one point. I thought she'd be better off without me. All she said was that she married me for better or worse and that meant the bad times as well as the good. She told me that to leave me would be the easy option, to throw me out and have our son back home. Nobody would object to that; it was just me they objected to. She wanted us to be together as a whole family not just half of one. All she had was her faith in Jesus and she believed with her whole heart that He would see us through. It was only after I was released that I realized that apart from God and one or two friends we stood alone.

We had access to our son any time we wanted, but to begin with Jo's parents had to be there at all times. It put a very big strain on all of us as I resented very much this part of it. This went on for a year. Then they said we could take him out on our own; we were allowed to take him to the park and anywhere else without her parents but he wasn't allowed to stay with us overnight unless Jo's parents were there. We all felt that this was a really ridiculous situation.

Time dragged on. It seemed as though we would never have our son home again. Some people may think that you can only mourn for the dead, but my sense of loss at this time was the same as for my children who had died. This was harder to deal with, because no matter where I went in the house, there was a reminder of him. There was an ache inside me that yearned for him; it wouldn't go away. It became worse each time we said goodbye to him and made the journey from London back to Margate. He tried to be so brave, not crying or letting us know he was upset. What a burden to place on such young shoulders. While we were trying to get him to show his feelings, Jo's mum and dad were telling him to be brave and not to upset us by crying. He bottled these feelings up for a long time. Fortunately he is beginning to release them now.

For the first time in my life I was beginning to feel normal. My problems were coming to the surface and I was dealing with them one by one. I was starting to con myself a little bit into believing that now my problems were being dealt with I could participate in the occasional social drink. I had been told that my emotional problems were the cause of my alcoholism and that when they were sorted out I would no longer have a problem with alcohol, allowing me to be a "normal" drinker. Peter Timms had told me he didn't agree with this theory and advised me against listening to it. I wanted nothing more than to be normal, so I went against his and Jo's advice and tried it.

I had a small drink to begin with, just a couple. I felt fine; they hadn't done me any harm. But it wasn't long before I was doing it again and this time I stayed out for most of the day. I didn't realize I was going backwards, that the doors were closing again and I stopped talking about my feelings. This went on for a couple of months and what started as social drinking soon became drinking binges which would last for nine or ten hours at a time. Then, however, because I was being counselled, I recognized the direction I was going in and with no excuses admitted why it was happening. Because I was able to do this I could stop just as quickly as I started. From then on I haven't looked back.

The battle with the authorities went on for two years and when finally the day came and we would have our say in court I wondered if it had all been worth it. All the pain and anguish I had gone through in coming to terms with my life – was it going to have been a waste of time? I began to feel as if it was all a game. There was no evidence that I'd ever harmed my son but who would believe me when I told them I wouldn't in the future? This was the day that would decide the future of our family.

We'd met the barrister beforehand. She wasn't like the Perry Masons of my past. She actually listened and took notice of us. We felt that with her help we had a chance.

On the train journey to the High Court on the first day I was nervous and full of trepidation. The only courts I'd ever been to before let me in but wouldn't let me out again and it was very hard to distinguish between the two. Jo kept telling me that this time was different, that God was with us and He was in control of the situation. Whatever happened it would be because He wanted it to.

We walked into the court building and my nerves really started to jangle. All I wanted to do was run, run as far away as I could where nobody could find me. Jo steadied me; she seemed to read my thoughts. She told me not to worry, that she would stay with me no matter what happened.

When we sat down in the courtroom I was surprised. It wasn't like others I'd been in – it was more informal. The judge wasn't wearing his robes, just a suit, and he looked quite ordinary. I braced myself for the onslaught that was to come and come it did. For three days they tore me to pieces, all of my past came out, my convictions, even my first marriage was brought up, no stone was left unturned. I was in conflict. Part of me believed that God would win and our son would come home, but the other side of me remembered my other court appearances when I was treated so unjustly and I thought we didn't stand a chance.

Towards the second half of the week things began to look up. It was now our turn to state our case. God really started to make His case to the court. Jo was called to give evidence and her answers were definitely God-inspired. She spoke with knowledge that defied her age – God had really scored points here. From then on I began to believe what Jo had told me all along – that we were going to win.

We were called back after the weekend for the final judgement. The nerves were jangling once again as we sat down and waited for the judge to go laboriously through the evidence an inch at a time. The barrister had told us on the Friday not to build up our hopes, but we couldn't help it. We knew God had something in store for us but we didn't know what form it would take. We hoped it would be the news we'd been waiting for for two years, so we made plans for our son's homecoming.

Then came the news we'd prayed for for so long – our little boy was coming home. I didn't know whether to laugh or cry. We were to be a whole family again. I didn't hear anything else that was said, I was too wrapped up in what I'd just heard.

We left the court on cloud nine. Jo and I just hugged each other. She couldn't get any sense out of me. I just kept repeating, "He's coming home."

I couldn't wait to tell him the good news and see the look on his face. We only realized how pure a child's faith is when he replied, "I knew I would. I've been saying goodbye to all my friends at school today." He didn't doubt God for one minute. Perhaps we could learn a lot from children.

Two days later we went to pick him up. He was already packed and ready to go. This was his big day and he wanted to get home as fast as he could. It was so different this time with him in the car with us. We kept thinking we had to take him back to his grandparents, then remembering that the next time he got out of the car would be in Margate, and home. This time it was a new beginning, and it would get better.

This episode in our lives took place just over two years ago. Since then the wardship has been discharged, which means that we are now once again John's fulltime parents. We have our son back, lock stock and barrel.

There have been over the past few years many people who have helped us. The church that we are involved with now, Holy Trinity in Margate, has been very supportive. The Anglican Church is now going to help me to go to college to gain the qualifications I need to carry out the work that God has given me to do. Without the friendship of these people, things might not have turned out quite so happily. I am now going from strength to strength, but it has not been without a lot of struggling at times. Through all my trials God has been there, but it took a lot of searching and prayer for me to get where I am now and to learn that the war I declared on God so long ago was one-sided. Also to learn that peace was just an arm's length away. I reached out my hand and He took it in His and I know He'll never let go. Neither will I.